Crochet

Learn It. Love It.

Techniques and Projects to Build a
Lifelong Passion, for Beginners Up

Search Press

Contents

Copyright © 2016, 2019
Quarto Publishing plc

This edition published in 2019 by
Search Press Ltd
Wellwood
North Farm Road
Tunbridge Wells
Kent TN2 3DR

ISBN: 978-1-78221-727-5

Conceived, designed and produced by:
Quarto Publishing plc
The Old Brewery
6 Blundell Street
London N7 9BH

QUAR.CCTH

Editor: Michelle Pickering
Art editor & designer: Jackie Palmer
Illustrator: Kuo Kang Chen
Picture researcher: Sarah Bell
Photographers: Nicki Dowey
  (location), Simon Pask (studio
model) and Phil Wilkins (techniques
  and swatches)
Editorial assistant: Georgia Cherry
Indexer: Diana LeCore
Art director: Caroline Guest
Creative director: Moira Clinch
Publisher: Paul Carslake

Printed in China

9 8 7 6 5 4 3 2 1

MIX
Paper from
responsible sources
FSC® C101537

Welcome ...

I come from a long line of enthusiastic crafters. My father had a talent for crochet, making lace doilies, dresses and blankets made up of hundreds of tiny motifs. He taught himself from a book and from a magazine that came in weekly parts. I would watch him and copy as he learned new stitches and techniques. I never imagined that one day I would make my living from this wonderful craft, designing for craft magazines and yarn suppliers.

In this book I have tried to pass on some of the skills that will help you to become a competent and confident crocheter. If you are a complete beginner, start with chapter 1, where you will find tips and helpful advice, from holding the hook and yarn to making your first crochet swatch. Later chapters gradually introduce more advanced techniques. If you have already mastered the basics, you will find these chapters full of advice and hints to take your crochet further.

Your crochet skills will improve with patience and practice. By following the step-by-step instructions and trying some of the quick start projects in this book, you will soon discover the creative opportunities crochet has to offer and will be making items you can be proud to give to your friends and family.

TRACEY TODHUNTER

About this book

This book explains all the core skills of crochet, from first picking up a hook to creating stitch patterns and achieving a professional finish. There are also plenty of practice patterns for swatches and projects.

CHAPTER 1
PAGES 8–53

The essential skills of crochet are explained here, from choosing yarn and hooks to working the basic stitches, joining in new colours, shaping techniques and finishing your crochet.

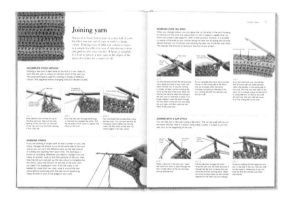

BE INSPIRED

Each chapter features a gallery of work from professional crochet designers, offering inspiration and information on how each piece was made.

CHAPTERS 2–5
PAGES 54–155

Once you know the basic stitches you can start to experiment, from working in the round (chapter 2) to combining stitches and creating exciting stitch patterns (chapter 3). Learn how to complete your work with a few finishing touches (chapter 4) and then explore some new techniques that will help you take your skills further (chapter 5).

Crochet clinics provide extra information and advice on solving common crochet dilemmas faced by beginners.

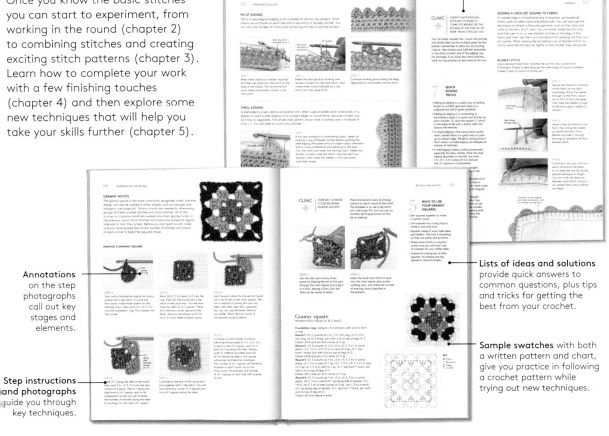

Annotations on the step photographs call out key stages and elements.

Step instructions and photographs guide you through key techniques.

Lists of ideas and solutions provide quick answers to common questions, plus tips and tricks for getting the best from your crochet.

Sample swatches with both a written pattern and chart, give you practice in following a crochet pattern while trying out new techniques.

QUICK START AND GUEST DESIGNER PROJECTS

Test your newfound skills with the projects found towards the end of each chapter. The quick start projects are designed to get you off the mark quickly and efficiently. The guest designer projects (see right) show you how talented, professional crochet designers work, and provide you with an opportunity to take your skills to a higher level.

The techniques featured in the book are highlighted at the start of each project, so that you can refer to the relevant technique when making the project.

Crochet charts are provided to complement the written pattern where it would be helpful to see a visual representation of the instructions.

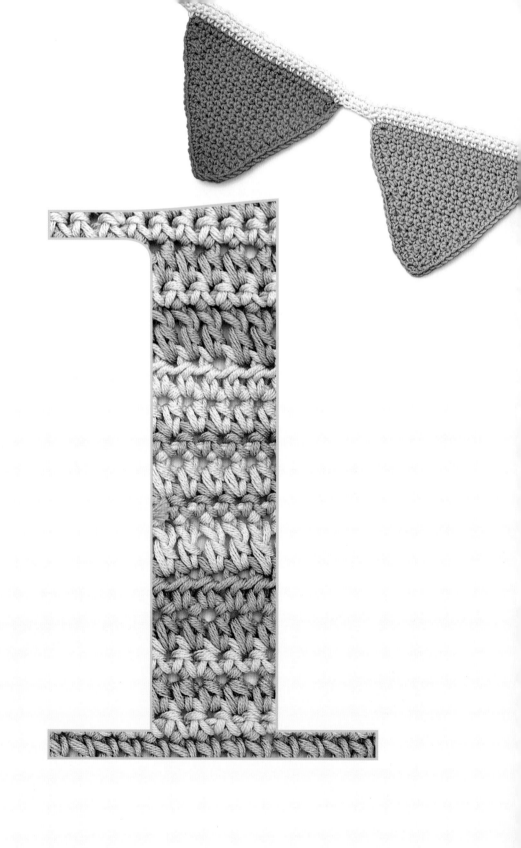

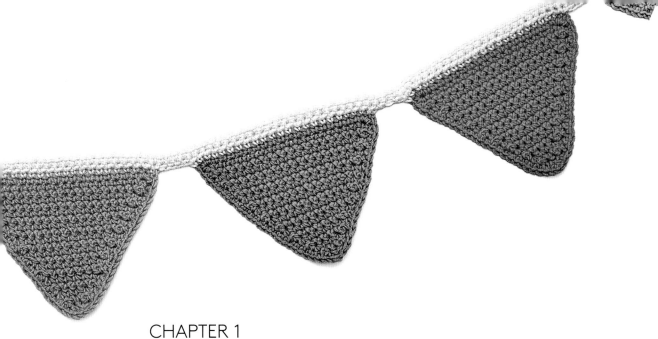

CHAPTER 1
Essential Skills

In this chapter you will learn the basic principles of crochet, such as choosing a hook and yarn, making chains and working the basic stitches. If you have never picked up a crochet hook before or you need to refresh your skills, this is the place to start. You will also find quick start projects designed to practise the basic techniques, as well advice on how to give your work a professional finish.

Yarn

Yarn is the generic term used to describe the material you crochet with. It can be a synthetic fibre such as acrylic, a natural fibre such as wool or a blend of different fibres. It is easy to be overwhelmed by the variety of yarns available, and knowing how to choose the right yarn for your project is a skill you will learn with experience. The ideal yarn for a beginner is a smooth (rather than textured) yarn in a single colour.

YARN TYPES

Yarn is presented either as a ready-wound ball or a wind-it-yourself hank. It may be manufactured from a single fibre – natural or synthetic – or a blend of several fibres. Confused by the variety of yarns available? Here is a guide to the most common yarns you will find in your local yarn shop.

WOOL

This is spun from sheep's fleece and is a natural fibre with a slight spring. Superwash wool is coated with synthetic microfibres that make it suitable for machine washing. The step-by-step instructions and quick start projects in this book use 100 per cent superwash DK (double-knitting) wool as it is smooth to work with and ideal for beginners.

wool

COTTON

A natural fibre, cotton produces fabric with good stitch definition and is suitable for beginners. It produces a durable fabric that is cool to wear.

cotton

ACRYLIC

A man-made fibre, sometimes labelled as microfibre, acrylic yarn is cheap and widely available. It is often combined with wool or cotton and can be a great budget choice for beginners or for larger items.

acrylic

ALPACA, MOHAIR AND ANGORA

Natural fibres spun from animals such as alpaca, goats and rabbits are becoming much more common and popular with yarn enthusiasts. They are sometimes a little fluffy, so it is best to wait until you have a little experience before experimenting with these yarns.

alpaca

SILK, BAMBOO AND LINEN

These natural fibres are often blended with other fibres, such as wool, to improve their elasticity and make them more suitable for crochet.

mohair

silk

linen

UNUSUAL MATERIALS

Of course, you can crochet with any material that comes to hand. Fine-tension wire can make beautiful crochet jewellery, and crochet cottons and threads are popular for fine lacework. In recent years, the interest in upcycling and recycling has led some enthusiasts to crochet with plastic bags cut into long strips, known as 'plarn'; this makes a strong, durable fabric. If you get the opportunity to experiment with different fibres, don't hesitate to try them out as the effects can be very pleasing and practical.

fine-gauge wire

YARN WEIGHTS

Yarn is generally categorised by the thickness of each strand, known as its weight. (Don't confuse this with the actual weight of the ball of yarn in grams or ounces.) Yarn weights range from lace, which is exceptionally fine, to jumbo, which hooks up into a thick, chunky fabric. The table below shows the most common weight categories and the names the yarns are usually known by, together with the usual tension range and hook sizes for each category.

 CLINIC I'VE NEVER BEEN IN A YARN SHOP BEFORE, AND THE CHOICE LOOKS SO OVERWHELMING. WHERE DO I START?

- **Take a list:** Be specific about what you need. For example, if you are buying yarn and tools to make one of the projects in this book, then take the book with you or make a note of what you need.
- **Ask for advice:** Most yarn shop staff are knitting or crochet enthusiasts and will be glad to help. They also want to encourage customers to become regular visitors, and offering practical advice, a warm welcome and yarns to suit all budgets is the best way to do this. If you don't find what you are looking for, go elsewhere. The same applies to shopping online. The world of online sales is very competitive and the best shops pride themselves on offering a personal service. Check out their blogs or social media to get an impression of how they treat their customers.
- **Start small:** To avoid expensive mistakes, start by buying a single ball (even if your project requires more), try it out and, if you like it, go back for the rest or try a different brand or yarn composition. As you become more experienced, you will discover which brands and yarn compositions you like best and can risk buying more than one ball.

Yarn weight category	Yarn weight names	Tension range to 10cm (4in)	Hook size range
0 LACE	2ply, fingering	32–42 dc	Steel 1.6–1.4mm; regular hook 2.25mm
1 SUPER FINE	Sock, fingering, baby	21–32 dc	2.25–3.5mm
2 FINE	4ply, sport, baby	16–20 dc	3.5–4.5mm
3 LIGHT	DK, light worsted	12–17 dc	4.5–5.5mm
4 MEDIUM	Aran, worsted, afghan	11–14 dc	5.5–6.5mm
5 BULKY	Chunky, craft, rug	8–11 dc	6.5–9mm
6 SUPER BULKY	Super chunky, roving	7–9 dc	9–15mm
7 JUMBO	Jumbo, roving	6 dc and fewer	15mm and larger

BALL BANDS

Most yarns come with a printed label that offers standard information on the fibre content, weight and aftercare. A standard ball band will provide the following information.

1 Name of yarn.
2 Yarn composition – which fibres have been used to make the yarn.
3 Weight of the ball – in grams and/or ounces.
4 Length of yarn – how many metres or yards are in the ball.
5 Recommended needle or hook size – usually given as a knitting needle size.
6 Tension – the number of stitches and rows you can expect over a 10cm (4in) square. Tension is usually given for a knitted square, but the information can be useful if you are trying to substitute the yarn recommended in your pattern.
7 Aftercare and washing instructions – pay special attention to the washing instructions. If you are making a gift, include a ball band with the finished item so that the recipient knows how to care for it.
8 Colour shade name or number and dye lot – the shade number corresponds to that given on the yarn company's shade card and may be specified in your pattern. Each batch of dye is given its own batch number and is produced in limited amounts. Because the shades can vary, always buy yarn with the same batch number if your pattern requires more than one ball.

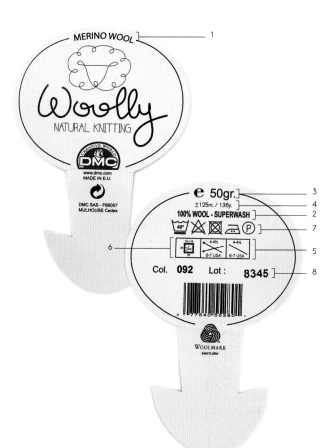

CLINIC

WHAT SHOULD I DO IF I CAN'T FIND THE YARN RECOMMENDED IN THE PATTERN?

If you are buying yarn for a particular project, it may not always be possible to buy the exact yarn specified in the pattern (it may have been discontinued, for example), or you may simply prefer to use a different yarn. In such cases, the information on the ball band should be your guide. Look for a yarn with a similar fibre content and weight (thickness). Next look for the same recommended hook size and a similar number of rows and stitches per 10cm (4in) square. Although no one can guarantee that your project will turn out exactly like the one in the pattern, these guidelines will help. If you choose a yarn from your stash (you will begin to collect a lot of yarn as your enthusiasm for crochet grows!), then the ball band may not be available. In this case, you should make a tension square to assess whether the yarn will be suitable (see page 30).

EMBELLISHMENTS

Once you begin to visit yarn and craft shops, you will soon start collecting small items to embellish your crochet projects. Buttons, beads and ribbon can add a professional finish to otherwise simple items. Novelty buttons for baby clothes, pretty ribbon trims on homewares and beads added to a simple crochet scarf will all add a personal touch. Many crocheters find they begin to accumulate lots of buttons, so a button tin to store them in is a useful purchase.

ERGONOMIC HOOK
This design can help reduce
strain on the wrist.

13

Equipment

Today's crocheter will have little difficulty finding crochet hooks and equipment – the hardest part is choosing what you really need and which style of tool will suit you best. Very little equipment is necessary for crochet – all you need is a hook, although items such as pins and sharp scissors are useful and relatively inexpensive. As you progress, you can collect more equipment as needed.

HOOKS

All crochet hooks are marked with their size, which refers to the diameter of the shank. The yarn you are using and the pattern you are working will determine which size hook to use. The size of the hook determines the size of your stitches. Most hooks are made from wood, plastic or aluminium. Some have a flat thumb rest or comfort grip; these are becoming more popular and are widely available in yarn and craft shops.

DOUBLE-ENDED HOOK
This has a different size
hook at each end.

CLINIC ⊹ HOW DO I KNOW WHICH HOOK TO CHOOSE?

Hooks are made of so many different materials and designs that it is a matter of personal choice. Some people find wooden or bamboo hooks warmer to hold, while steel or aluminium can feel cold or hard. You can also buy ergonomic hooks and comfort grips that are designed for comfort and reduced strain on the wrist. Try as many hooks as you can before buying, and ask for advice in your local yarn shop. They often have samples you can try before making a purchase.

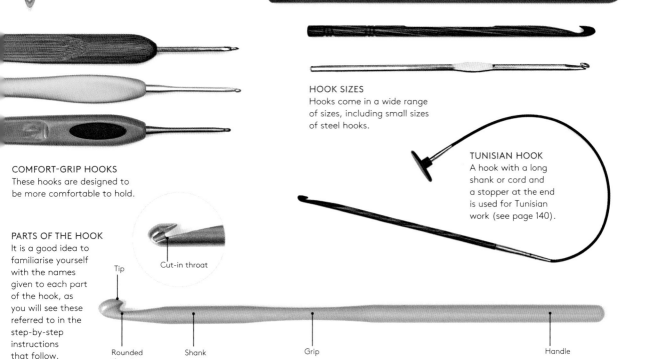

HOOK SIZES
Hooks come in a wide range
of sizes, including small sizes
of steel hooks.

TUNISIAN HOOK
A hook with a long
shank or cord and
a stopper at the end
is used for Tunisian
work (see page 140).

COMFORT-GRIP HOOKS
These hooks are designed to
be more comfortable to hold.

PARTS OF THE HOOK
It is a good idea to familiarise yourself with the names given to each part of the hook, as you will see these referred to in the step-by-step instructions that follow.

Tip

Cut-in throat

Rounded throat

Shank

Grip

Handle

ACCESSORIES

In addition to hooks and yarn, the following equipment will make your life easier and become more essential as you progress. You may already have some of them in your craft supplies at home; others you will need to buy. They are all available from craft shops.

SCISSORS

A small, sharp pair of scissors is essential for cutting yarn and trimming yarn ends.

TAPE MEASURE OR RULER

You will need to measure your work. A metal ruler or tape measure is best because fabric measures can stretch. Choose a retractable tape measure for convenience.

TAPESTRY NEEDLE

Available in a range of sizes, a tapestry or yarn needle with a blunt end and large eye is used for weaving in ends and sewing seams.

STITCH MARKERS

Look out for split ring or locking markers that are designed specifically for crochet. They can be clipped and unclipped to mark stitches or to indicate the beginning of a round. A safety pin can be used instead, but the sharp point can split your work, so use with caution.

ROW COUNTER

This is useful for counting rows or pattern repeats and can be bought in most craft or yarn shops.

DRESSMAKER'S PINS

You will find a small supply of pins useful for blocking your work (the process of finishing your project so that the seams lie straight and flat) and for sewing seams. Buy ones that will not rust.

5 TOOLS YOU'LL NEED TO GET STARTED

It can be tempting to rush out and buy lots of new gadgets and tools for your new hobby. To make sure you spend your money wisely, here is a list of what you really need.

1 Crochet hook – the quick start projects in this book use a 4mm hook, so make that your first purchase.

2 Scissors – any pair will do for now.

3 Tape measure

4 Tapestry needle

5 Bag to put everything in – a pencil case will do a great job of keeping all your tools together. Craft shops sell a huge range of craft bags and workboxes.

BOBBINS

You will need to wind off small balls of yarn when working intarsia designs in multiple colours (see page 107). Winding the yarn on to bobbins will help to keep it tangle-free.

PENCIL AND NOTEBOOK

Some would argue that these are essential. Keep a notebook in your workbag for keeping track of where you are in a pattern or for making notes of designs you like in books or magazines.

5 **LITTLE LUXURIES** A quick walk around your local craft shop will reveal dozens of gadgets that you don't need, but that are useful additions to your toolkit. Buy them only when, and if, you need them.

1 **Ball winder and swift:** These definitely fall into the luxury category. They are used for winding hanks of yarn into a ball. They can make your life easier, but most yarn shops will be happy to wind hanks of yarn that you purchase from them.

2 **Pompom makers:** Pompoms are very easy to make using circles of cardboard, but these small plastic tools are quick and easy to use. Buy a few in different sizes to suit the type of work you like doing.

3 **Yarn bowl:** This is what it sounds like – a large bowl, generally ceramic or wood, to hold your yarn. These bowls usually have a hook or hole cut out of the side to feed the yarn through and keep it from rolling around on the floor while you work (this can make it dusty or tangled). There are many styles available. A small plastic tub will do the job just as well.

4 **Daylight lamps:** If you often crochet in the evening or use dark colours, a daylight bulb can make it much easier to see your work. A variety of lamps and bulbs are available to suit your budget. It is best to try them out first, so ask advice in your local craft shop or ask for recommendations among your friends before purchasing.

5 **Blocking boards and wires:** When you begin to make larger items, such as shawls and garments, blocking wires are a helpful way to achieve a professional finish. These are lengths of special stainless steel wire that are threaded through the edges of the piece of crochet to keep them straight. Some crocheters never use them; others think they are essential. Your local yarn shop may have a set you can try out before you invest. Blocking boards are usually made of foam and are ideal for pinning out fabric. Some have a square grid that is helpful for pinning out shapes and motifs with accuracy. You will find more information on blocking on page 42, so don't worry if you are unfamiliar with this term.

Getting started

The first step in crochet is learning to handle the hook and yarn in a comfortable way. The two most common ways of holding them are demonstrated here, but there is no right or wrong way – comfort and manoeuvrability are what matter. To start making a crochet fabric, you need to make a slip knot on the hook and then work a foundation chain – this is the equivalent of casting on in knitting.

HOLDING AND TENSIONING THE YARN

When you hold the yarn, there should be some tension between the working yarn (the yarn coming from the ball) and the hook. This allows your hand to move freely as you make each stitch, and allows you more control as you wrap the yarn over the hook. The particular method you use is not important, but it is worth trying both methods pictured here. You will soon find a way that feels most comfortable to you. Try to stay relaxed, sit comfortably and don't grip the hook too tightly.

INDEX FINGER METHOD

Working yarn going to hook

STEP 1
Wrap the working yarn around the little finger of your left hand, pass it under your ring and middle fingers and then bring it up over your index finger.

STEP 2
Holding the chain or piece of crochet steady between the thumb and middle finger of your left hand, and with the hook in your right hand, use your left index finger to raise the yarn over the hook and control the tension of the yarn.

MIDDLE FINGER METHOD

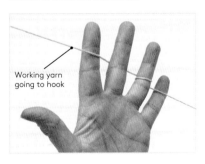

Working yarn going to hook

STEP 1
Some crocheters prefer to control the working yarn with their middle finger, so that their index finger is free to hold the crochet. Wrap the yarn around either the left ring finger or little finger and then bring it up over your middle finger. This is the method you will see in many of the photographs in this book.

STEP 2
Holding the chain or crochet steady between your left thumb and index finger, and the hook in your right hand, use your left middle finger to raise the yarn over the hook and control the tension of the yarn.

HOLDING THE HOOK

PEN METHOD
Hold the hook as you would a pen, between your index finger and thumb. Hold the hook about 2.5cm (1in) from the throat of the hook. If the hook has a comfort grip, your thumb should rest on it.

KNIFE METHOD
Hold the hook overhand as you would a knife, with your index finger about 2.5cm (1in) from the throat.

MAKING A SLIP KNOT

All crochet starts by making a loop on the hook. The first loop on the hook is usually made with a slip knot, which anchors the yarn to the hook. If you knit, you will be familiar with making a slip knot to begin casting on. You can use the same method for crochet.

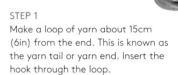

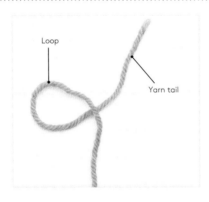

Loop

Yarn tail

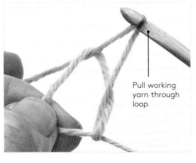

STEP 1
Make a loop of yarn about 15cm (6in) from the end. This is known as the yarn tail or yarn end. Insert the hook through the loop.

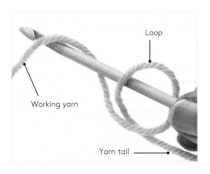

Loop

Working yarn

Yarn tail

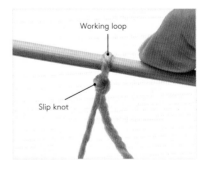

Pull working yarn through loop

Working loop

Slip knot

STEP 2
Wrap the working yarn (the yarn coming from the ball) over the hook and then draw it through the loop.

STEP 3
This makes a loop on the hook.

STEP 4
Tighten the slip knot by pulling gently on the yarn tail and then you are ready to make your first crochet stitches. The loop on the hook is called the working loop. Do not pull the working loop too tightly; you need to be able to move it along the shaft of the hook as you work.

MAKING A FOUNDATION CHAIN

A length of chains, or chain stitches, forms the foundation of the crochet fabric, and your first row of crochet stitches will be worked into this foundation chain. Chains can also be used for decorative effect within the body of the crochet fabric, such as for lacework. Practise making chains until the motion of wrapping the yarn over the hook feels comfortable and you are able to make chains that are even in size.

Slip knot forms first working loop

STEP 1
Make a slip knot on the hook and hold the base of the slip knot with your right fingers.

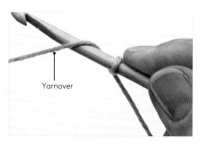

Yarnover

STEP 2
Wrap the working yarn from back to front over the hook. This known as a yarnover and is abbreviated to 'yo' in patterns.

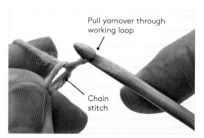

Pull yarnover through working loop

Chain stitch

STEP 3
Draw the yarn through the loop on the hook to complete your first chain.

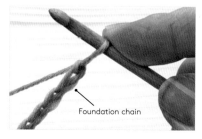

Foundation chain

STEP 4
Continue making chains in this way until you have the number specified in the pattern. In crochet patterns, the chain is abbreviated to 'ch'.

COUNTING THE CHAINS

It is important that the foundation chain contains the required number of chain stitches for the pattern you will be working. If you look closely at the foundation chain, you will see that there is a noticeable front and back. The front of the chain looks like a series of V shapes; the back has a distinct bump of yarn behind each V.

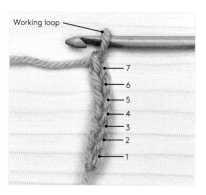

Working loop

FROM THE FRONT
Lay the chain on a flat surface with the front uppermost. The loop on the hook – the working loop – does not count as a stitch. Count each V as one chain. You may find it easier to count from the slip knot towards the hook. That way, if you need to remove or add chains, you don't have to start counting from scratch.

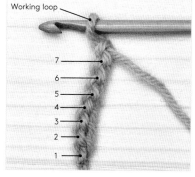

Working loop

FROM THE BACK
Some people find it easier to turn the foundation chain over and count the back bumps. Try both methods and see which one suits you best.

WORKING INTO THE FOUNDATION CHAIN

The first row of crochet stitches is worked into the foundation chain. The hook can be inserted into the chain in different ways. The most common method, and the easiest one for a beginner, is to work through the front of the chain. Working into the front of the chain produces a looser edge, while working into the back produces a stronger edge.

Top loop

Bottom loop

Back bump

THROUGH THE FRONT

This is the most common method and is used throughout this book unless specified otherwise. Holding the chain with the front facing you, insert the hook under the top loop of the chain stitch – that is, under the left-hand leg of the V shape – and then work the crochet stitch instructed in the pattern.

THROUGH THE BACK

Turn the chain so that the back is facing you. Insert the hook under the bump on the back of the chain stitch.

5

COMMON CHAIN PROBLEMS AND HOW TO SOLVE THEM

1 Keep count of chains by inserting a stitch marker every 10th stitch. This makes it easier to keep track.

2 Prevent your chain from twisting by always inserting the hook under the top loop of the V shape on the front of the chain.

3 If you find that your chain is too tight, try making each yarnover slightly longer, or use a hook one size larger for the foundation chain and then switch back to the recommended hook size for working the pattern.

4 When you first begin to crochet, it can be difficult to make the correct number of chains. If you make too many, the extra chains can be unpicked from the slip knot end after you have worked a few rows.

5 If you have too few chains, you can work extra chains using the tail end of the yarn. Insert the hook into the end chain and, using this as a stitch, make the required number of extra chains using the yarn tail.

FASTENING OFF

Before you continue learning how to crochet, you need to know how to fasten off the yarn to secure it and stop it from unravelling.

Yarn tail

STEP 1
After you have practised making a foundation chain, cut the yarn, leaving a 15cm (6in) tail.

STEP 2
Draw the tail of yarn through the remaining loop on the hook, then pull tight to fasten. The same method can be used to fasten off any piece of crochet you make.

CLINIC

✚

I'M LEFT-HANDED. CAN I STILL LEARN TO CROCHET?

Yes, you can. Although most instruction books and patterns are written with right-handed crochet in mind, you can adapt the instructions to suit you. Some left-handers who can already knit find that they can follow the directions and crochet with the hook in their right hand. If this does not work for you, then try holding the hook and yarn as described in this book but using the opposite hands. Hold a mirror up to the step-by-step photographs in the book so that the direction is reversed. You can also find online tutorials and videos designed for left-handed crocheters.

Working the basic stitches

This section introduces the basic stitches that are used to create any crochet fabric. They are all worked using the same principle, the difference being the finished height of each stitch. They range from slip stitch and double crochet, the shortest stitches, and progress through half trebles and trebles to the more unusual taller stitches, such as the double treble and triple treble.

Double crochet

Half treble crochet

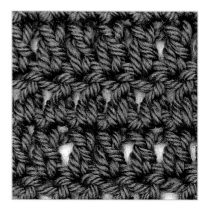

Treble crochet

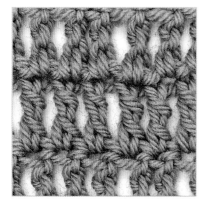

Double treble crochet

Triple treble crochet

BASIC CROCHET STITCHES

These five swatches show the basic stitches that are used to make crochet fabrics (slip stitch performs other functions; see page 22). Double crochet and treble crochet are the two most commonly used stitches. Each swatch is shown actual size to give you an idea of the relative scale of each stitch, ranging from the solid, dense fabric of double crochet to the very loose and open triple treble crochet.

4 THINGS TO REMEMBER ABOUT COUNTING STITCHES

1 Count each V along the top of the last row of crochet as one stitch.

2 Don't count the loop on the hook.

3 Count the turning chain at the beginning of the row as one stitch except on double crochet fabric, when you should ignore the turning chain, unless a pattern specifies otherwise (see page 22).

4 Try to get into the habit of counting the number of stitches regularly, ideally after finishing each row, to make sure you have the correct number.

Back loop of V
Front loop of V

Top of stitch – this is the view you will see when you have just completed a row, with two loops forming a V shape at the top of each stitch; insert the crochet hook under both loops of this V when working a new stitch unless specified otherwise in the pattern (see page 84)

Top of stitch – this is the view you will see when you turn the work, ready to begin a new row; the V shape at the top is not visible from this angle, so tilt the work to allow you to insert the hook under both loops of the V when working each stitch

Space between stitches – sometimes a pattern may tell you to insert the hook into this space to work the next stitch instead of under the top V loops

V shape at top of stitches

Fastened off here

6 rows of double crochet (2 rows in each colour)

2 rows of treble crochet

6 rows of double crochet (2 rows in each colour)

Post (or stem) of stitch – the height of the post varies, depending on the stitch; sometimes a pattern will instruct you to work a stitch around the post instead of under the top V loops (see page 86)

Turning chain – chain stitches are worked at the beginning of a row to bring the hook up to the correct height for the stitch you will be working next (see page 22)

Row 1 starts here – all rows are worked from right to left, with the work turned between rows; the first row usually forms the right side of the fabric but not always

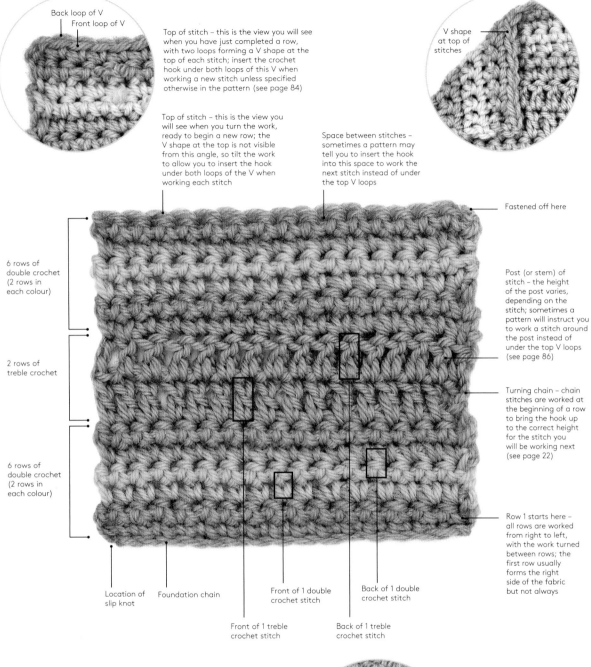

Location of slip knot

Foundation chain

Front of 1 treble crochet stitch

Front of 1 double crochet stitch

Back of 1 treble crochet stitch

Back of 1 double crochet stitch

UNDERSTANDING CROCHET STITCHES

This swatch has been worked in the two most commonly used crochet stitches: double crochet and treble crochet. Learning some basic terminology and how to recognise the stitches and the way they link together to form the finished fabric will be helpful when you start learning how to work the basic stitches.

Yarn tail – after finishing the crochet, any ends of yarn need to be woven through the back of stitches for a neat finish (see page 40)

UNDERSTANDING TURNING CHAINS

A number of chain stitches are needed at the beginning of each row of crochet to bring the hook up to the same height as the first stitch you will be working in order keep the edges of the work straight. These chains are included in the foundation chain for the first row, but must be added on subsequent rows. They are known as a turning chain because they are made when the work is turned to start the new row. (When working in the round, they are called a starting chain since you do not turn the work.)

HOW MANY CHAINS?

Since the different crochet stitches vary in height, you have to make a different number of chains for each type of stitch. The list below and the diagram on the right show the number of chains usually made for the basic stitches, but the pattern should always tell you how many to make.

- Double crochet (dc) = 1 turning chain
- Half treble crochet (htr) = 2 turning chains
- Treble crochet (tr) = 3 turning chains
- Double treble crochet (dtr) = 4 turning chains
- Triple treble crochet (trtr) = 5 turning chains
- For taller stitches, keep adding 1 extra turning chain

DO THEY COUNT AS A STITCH?

The pattern will tell you if the turning chain counts as a stitch, but as a general rule, the turning chain counts as the first stitch of the new row, except for double crochet, when it is usually not counted. When working some stitch patterns, the turning chain may be longer than the number required for the stitch, in which case it counts for the first stitch plus the number of extra chains – for example, 5 turning chains count as 1 treble crochet plus 2 chains.

AT THE BEGINNING OR END OF A ROW?

It does not matter if you make the turning chains before or after you turn the work, but it is a good idea to be consistent.

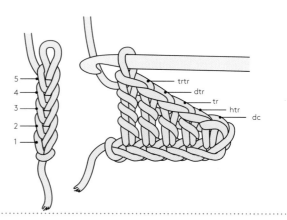

SLIP STITCH

A slip stitch (abbreviated to 'sl st' in patterns) adds virtually no height and is rarely used to create a crochet fabric. Instead it is used to move the hook and yarn across one or more existing stitches to a new position without adding any height. It is also used to join the ends of a foundation chain to make a ring for working in the round (see page 56), or to make an invisible join in a stitch pattern.

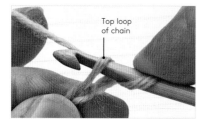

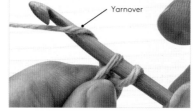

STEP 1
Insert the hook into the chain or stitch specified in the pattern. Here, the hook is inserted into the second chain from the hook on a foundation chain. Insert the hook under the top loop of the chain, just as when working a chain stitch.

STEP 2
Wrap the yarn over the hook.

STEP 3
Draw the yarn through the chain and the loop on the hook to complete the slip stitch. Note that no turning chain is required when working a slip stitch at the beginning of a row.

DOUBLE CROCHET

This is considered the easiest of the stitches that are used to create the main body of a crochet fabric and forms the basis for all the taller stitches that follow. It creates a tight, dense fabric and can be used to make garments, toys and homewares. Take your time to master double crochet (abbreviated to 'dc' in patterns) and you will find it much easier to learn the other stitches.

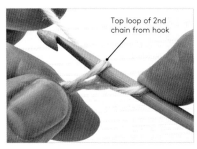

STEP 1
Make a foundation chain and hold it with the front (the V side) of the chain facing you. Locate the second chain from the hook and insert the hook under the top loop of the chain.

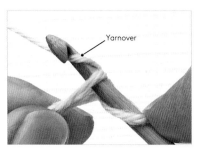

STEP 2
Wrap the yarn over the hook from back to front.

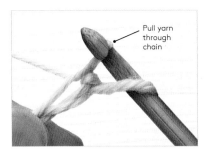

STEP 3
Gently draw the loop of yarn through the chain. You will find it easier to do this if the hook is turned slightly towards you. There are now two loops on the hook.

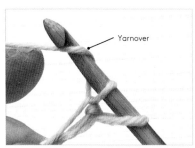

STEP 4
Wrap the yarn over the hook again.

STEP 5
Draw the yarn through both loops on the hook to complete your first double crochet stitch.

STEP 6
Continue across the foundation chain, working a double crochet into each chain. This first row of stitches is sometimes referred to as the foundation row.

STEP 7
Each row of crochet is worked from right to left, so once you have reached the end of the row, you need to turn the work in order to begin the next row. Turn the work over as if turning the page of a book. Then make one chain for the turning chain to bring the hook up to the height of the double crochet stitches you are working (see page 22).

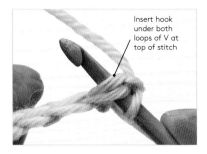

STEP 8
Work the first double crochet into the top of the first stitch on the row below. Each completed crochet stitch has two loops of yarn lying flat along the top (it looks like the V of a chain stitch). Always insert the hook under both legs of the V unless specified otherwise in the pattern. Continue working double crochet stitches across the row.

HALF TREBLE CROCHET

This is a slightly taller stitch than double crochet and is worked using the same basic principle. Half treble crochet stitch creates a fabric with a soft, dense texture. In patterns, it is abbreviated to 'htr'.

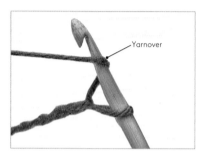

STEP 1
Hold the foundation chain with the front facing you. Wrap the yarn over the hook from back to front.

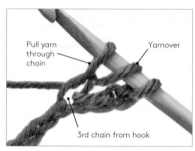

STEP 2
Insert the hook under the top loop of the third chain from the hook. Catch the yarn with the hook and draw it through the chain, so that you now have three loops on the hook.

STEP 3
Wrap the yarn over the hook again and draw it through all three loops on the hook to complete your first half treble crochet stitch. Continue across the foundation chain, working a half treble into each chain.

STEP 4
Once you have reached the end of the row, turn the work to begin the next row. Make two chains for the turning chain. This counts as the first stitch of the row. Work a half treble into the top of the second stitch on the row below, making sure that you insert the hook under both legs of the V that lies at the top of the stitch.

STEP 5
Continue working half treble crochet stitches across the row.

STEP 6
When you reach the end of the row, work the last half treble into the top of the two chain stitches at the beginning of the first row. On subsequent rows, the last stitch is made into the top of the turning chain of the previous row.

TREBLE CROCHET

Treble crochet follows the same principles as the previous stitches. Treble crochet is the most commonly used crochet stitch and makes an open, loose fabric. It is also reversible (meaning it looks the same on the front and the back). In crochet patterns, it is abbreviated to 'tr'.

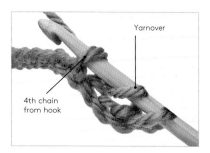

STEP 1
Hold the foundation chain with the front of the chain facing you. Wrap the yarn over the hook from back to front, then insert the hook under the top loop of the fourth chain from the hook.

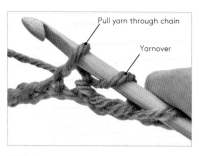

STEP 2
Catch the yarn with the hook and draw a loop through the chain. Now you have three loops on the hook.

STEP 3
Wrap the yarn over the hook again and draw it through the first two loops on the hook.

STEP 4
Wrap the yarn over the hook again and draw it through the two remaining loops on the hook. This completes your first treble crochet stitch.

STEP 5
Continue across the foundation chain, working a treble crochet into each chain to complete the first row.

STEP 6
Turn the work ready to begin the next row and make three chains for the turning chain. This counts as the first stitch of the row.

STEP 7
Work a treble into the top of the second stitch on the row below, making sure that you insert the hook under both legs of the V that lies at the top of the stitch. Continue working treble crochet stitches across the row. When you reach the end of the row, work the last treble crochet into the top of the three chain stitches at the beginning of the first row. On subsequent rows, the last stitch is made into the top of the turning chain of the previous row.

DOUBLE TREBLE CROCHET

Once you have mastered double, half treble and treble crochet, you should begin to understand how wrapping the yarn over the hook is the principle of making taller stitches. Double treble crochet is a tall stitch with a very loose texture and is abbreviated to 'dtr' in patterns.

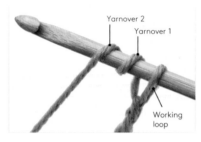

STEP 1
Hold the foundation chain with the front of the chain facing you. Wrap the yarn over the hook from back to front twice.

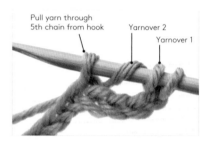

STEP 2
Insert the hook under the top loop of the fifth chain from the hook. Catch the yarn with the hook and draw a loop of yarn through the chain, so that you now have four loops on the hook.

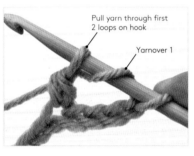

STEP 3
Wrap the yarn over the hook again and draw it through the first two loops on the hook, leaving three loops on the hook.

STEP 4
Wrap the yarn over the hook again and draw it through two loops, leaving two loops on the hook.

STEP 5
Wrap the yarn over the hook once more and draw it through the last two loops on the hook. You have completed your first double treble crochet stitch.

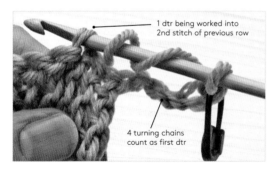

STEP 6
Continue across the foundation chain, working a double treble crochet into each chain. When you reach the end of the row, turn the work and make four chains for the turning chain (the top of the turning chain is marked with a stitch marker here; see clinic opposite). This counts as the first stitch of the row. Work a double treble into the top of the second stitch on the row below, making sure that you insert the hook under both legs of the V that lies at the top of the stitch.

STEP 7
Continue working double treble crochet stitches across the row. When you reach the end of the row, work the last double treble crochet into the top of the four chain stitches at the beginning of the first row. On subsequent rows, the last stitch is made into the top of the turning chain of the previous row (marked here with a stitch marker).

TRIPLE TREBLE CROCHET

This tall stitch is abbreviated to 'trtr' in patterns. It follows the same principle as double treble crochet, but you start by wrapping the yarn over the hook three times instead of twice. You can make even taller stitches – quadruple treble, quintuple treble and so on – using the same principle of wrapping the yarn over the hook an extra time and then drawing it through the loops on the hook in pairs.

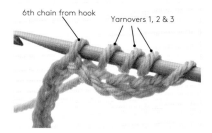

6th chain from hook   Yarnovers 1, 2 & 3

STEP 1
Begin by wrapping the yarn three times over the hook. Insert the hook under the top loop of the sixth chain from the hook.

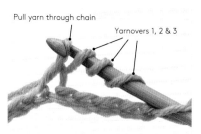

Pull yarn through chain   Yarnovers 1, 2 & 3

STEP 2
Catch the yarn with the hook and draw it through the chain so that you have five loops on the hook.

Pull yarn through first 2 loops on hook

STEP 3
Wrap the yarn over the hook again and draw it through the first two loops, leaving four loops on the hook.

First row of trtr being worked

STEP 4
Continue to wrap the yarn over the hook and draw it through two loops at a time until the stitch is complete and you only have one loop on the hook. Continue working triple trebles across the chain. When turning the work to start subsequent rows, make six turning chains and work the first triple treble into the second stitch on the previous row. Work the last triple treble of each row into the top of the turning chain.

CLINIC

HELP! ON EVERY ROW I HAVE FEWER STITCHES THAN THE ROW BEFORE. WHAT AM I DOING WRONG?

Learning how to count stitches is a vital part of successful crochet (see page 20). On the taller stitches, a decreasing stitch count is often caused by not working the last stitch of the row into the top of the turning chain of the previous row. To help you identify where to work the last stitch, insert a stitch marker into the last chain of the turning chain when you make it (as demonstrated opposite). On the next row, work the final stitch of the row into the marked chain. Keep moving the marker to the last chain of the turning chain when you start subsequent rows.

TALLER AND TALLER
By wrapping the yarn over the hook as many times as you wish before inserting the hook into the chain or stitch, it is possible to make crochet stitches as tall as you like.

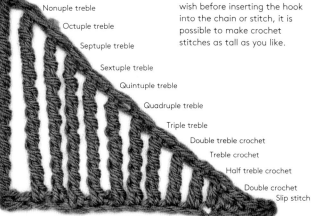

Decuple treble
Nonuple treble
Octuple treble
Septuple treble
Sextuple treble
Quintuple treble
Quadruple treble
Triple treble
Double treble crochet
Treble crochet
Half treble crochet
Double crochet
Slip stitch

Reading patterns and charts

Crochet patterns can look complicated and intimidating, but once you understand the basic terminology and abbreviations, following a pattern will soon become easier. Crochet pattern instructions can be written line by line, or shown in visual form as a chart. Sometimes a pattern will have both types of instructions. You will find a list of the crochet abbreviations and chart symbols used throughout this book on page 156.

THINGS A PATTERN SHOULD TELL YOU

As well as a set of instructions for crocheting, a pattern should supply you with the following:

1 Size of the finished item (there may be multiple sizes for garments).

2 Tension of the piece.

3 Yarn and any other materials required.

4 Recommended hook size.

5 Abbreviations used in the instructions, including an explanation of how to work any unusual ones.

DECODING A WRITTEN PATTERN

Crochet patterns use standard conventions and abbreviations to save space and avoid repetition. Read through the following information, then try following the sample pattern opposite.

ABBREVIATIONS

Most patterns will give you a list of abbreviations used in the pattern. This can help you to decide if the pattern is suitable for your level of experience. Although many abbreviations are standardised, such as 'ch' for chain, some of them vary, so always read the abbreviations for the pattern you are making before starting to crochet.

PATTERN REPEATS

Square brackets and asterisks are used to avoid repetition and make a pattern shorter. Square brackets [ ] are used to denote small repeats, such as '[2 dc, 3 tr, 2 dc] twice', whereas asterisks are used to mark the beginning of a section that should be repeated. For example, '[1 dc in each of next 2 sts, ch 1] 3 times' means that you should make one double crochet into each of the next two stitches, then make one chain, a total of three times. The same instruction using asterisks would read '*1 dc in each of next 2 sts, ch 1; repeat from * twice'. The instruction is the same, but it is written in a slightly different way. In the asterisk example, the instruction should be worked once, then repeated the number of times indicated after the asterisk.

Where the instructions given after the asterisk do not fit exactly, or if a different stitch is worked at the end of the row or round, the instructions may read, for example: '*1 dc in each of next 2 sts, ch 1, 2 dc in next st; repeat from * ending 1 dc in last st'. This means that you should repeat the instructions after the asterisk, but at the end of the last repeat, you should work only one double crochet in the last stitch.

ADDITIONAL INFORMATION

Parentheses (curved brackets) are used to show when a string of stitches are worked in the same place, for example: '(1 dc, 1 htr, 1 dc) in next st'. They are also used to provide information rather than instructions. One of the most usual is '(RS)' after a row number, which indicates that this row is the right side of the work. Another is '(counts as)' after the turning chain instruction. For example, 'ch 5 (counts as 1 tr, ch 2)' means that the five chain stitches count as one treble crochet, plus two extra chains.

At the end of each row, stitch counts are usually given inside parentheses. A pattern written for more than one size may have larger sizes or stitch counts for each size given inside parentheses.

CHAIN MULTIPLES

The beginning of the pattern will tell you how many chains to make before starting the first row. This will usually be a specific number, but occasionally you may be instructed to work over a multiple (this is often the case in stitch dictionaries and you will also find this instruction in the sample swatch patterns in chapter 3 of this book). If a pattern tells you to make 'a multiple of 3 ch + 2', this does not mean a multiple of 5. Instead, you are being asked to work a multiple of three chains – 3, 6, 9 and so on – and then add an extra two chains – 3 + 2, 6 + 2, 9 + 2 and so on.

Mock bobbles

This pattern combines two basic stitches of different heights. The taller double trebles are pulled down by the double crochets on either side of them to create the effect of small bobbles.

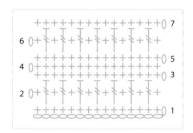

Foundation chain: Make an even number of ch.
Row 1: 1 dc in second ch from hook, 1 dc in each ch to end, turn.
Row 2: Ch 1, 1 dc in first st, *1 dtr in next st, 1 dc in next st; rep from * to end, turn.
Rows 3–5: Ch 1, 1 dc in each st to end, turn.
Repeat rows 2–5 for pattern.

KEY
◯ Chain
+ Double crochet
⌡ Double treble crochet

DECODING A CHART
Sometimes a crochet pattern will be accompanied by a chart, which can give a helpful visual interpretation of the written pattern. There are several different types of crochet chart, but each will be accompanied by a key to explain any symbols used.

SYMBOL CHARTS
Symbol charts are used to describe the work visually and show where stitches should be placed in relation to each other. Charts give an immediate visual impression of what the finished piece will look like. Each symbol represents a single stitch or instruction. Some crocheters prefer to work from charts as they can visualise their work more clearly. Some prefer a combination of both written and chart instructions.

In order to decode a chart, you need to become familiar with crochet symbols. The panel above shows the chart and written instructions for a mock bobbles swatch. On the chart you can see where each stitch should be made, the direction of work and the number of rows.

Charts for working in rows have numbers at each side to indicate the row numbers, normally beginning with row 1 at the bottom. Right side rows are numbered at the right of the chart, and

are read from right to left. Wrong side rows are numbered at the left, and are read from left to right – that is, read each row starting at the edge where the number appears. Charts for working in rounds begin from the centre, and each round is usually numbered close to where the round begins. Unless indicated otherwise, each round should be read anticlockwise, to match the direction of work.

When you are working from a chart, you may find it easier to make an enlarged copy using a photocopier and mark off each row or round as it is completed.

COLOUR BLOCK CHARTS
Tapestry and intarsia patterns are usually worked from a coloured chart on a grid rather than from rows of written instructions. Each coloured square on the grid represents one stitch, and you should always work upwards from the

bottom. A key will accompany the chart to indicate which yarn is represented by which chart colour. See pages 106–107 for more information.

FILET CHARTS
Filet is a special form of crochet that often comes without written instructions. The charts are similar to cross stitch charts, with small dots or filled squares indicating where stitches should be made. See page 95 for more information.

SCHEMATICS
Many modern crochet garment patterns will also include a schematic. This is an outline drawing showing where important measurements should be taken. This can also help you pin out garment pieces to the correct size before blocking or pressing, and will show you where shaping is made, such as waistlines or sleeves.

Tension

Tension refers to the number of stitches and rows to a given measurement, usually 10cm (4in) square. It is essential that your crochet matches the tension specified in the pattern if your finished piece is to be the correct size. Tension is affected by many things: the type of yarn, the size and brand of crochet hook, the stitch pattern being used and your own individual way of working.

CLINIC : MY STITCH COUNT IS ACCURATE, BUT I HAVE TOO FEW ROWS TO MATCH THE TENSION. WHAT SHOULD I DO?

As a general rule, it is more important to achieve an accurate stitch count, but there are a few things you can do to achieve a more accurate row count.

- Changing the size of your hook can sometimes help to fix an inaccurate row tension without affecting the number of stitches.
- Try using a hook made of a different material or adjusting your technique. It may be that you have too few rows because you are drawing up each loop too loosely, or too many rows because you are sitting in an uncomfortable position and making the stitches too tight.
- If, despite all your attempts, you cannot achieve an accurate row count, you may have to adjust the number of rows you work in the pattern, such as working more or fewer rows before the armhole shaping on a jumper.

MEASURING YOUR TENSION

Using the yarn, hook size and stitch recommended in the tension instruction of the pattern, work a generously sized test swatch. If the specified tension is measured over a 10cm (4in) square, for example, then make a swatch 15–20cm (6–8in) square. Block the test swatch (see page 42) or let it rest for a while so that the stitches can relax.

STEP 1
Place the swatch on a flat surface and use a metal ruler to measure 10cm (4in) across a row of stitches. Mark each end of this measurement with a pin. Count the number of stitches between the pins, including any partial stitches, to calculate your stitch tension.

STEP 2
Measure the row tension by placing the ruler vertically and marking 10cm (4in) with pins. Count the number of rows between the pins, including any partial rows, to calculate your row tension.

STEP 3
When working a repeated stitch pattern, the tension information may be quoted as a multiple of the pattern repeat, rather than as a set number of stitches and rows. For example, '8 pattern repeats = 9cm (3½in)'. Use a ruler to measure this distance and mark it with pins, then count the number of repeats between the pins.

ADJUSTING YOUR TENSION

If your tension is different from that specified in the pattern,
you need to change the size of hook you are using.
- Too many stitches or pattern repeats – your tension is too tight,
  so try again using a larger hook.
- Too few stitches or pattern repeats – your tension is too loose,
  so try again using a smaller hook.

Continue making and measuring tension swatches, adjusting the
hook by one size each time, until you achieve the required tension.

SAME YARN, DIFFERENT HOOK SIZE
The two treble crochet swatches below are worked in DK-weight wool yarn,
using a 3.5mm hook (left) and a 4.5mm hook (right).

The details above
show the stitches
at actual size; the
swatches on the
left are shown at
25 per cent.

SAME HOOK SIZE, DIFFERENT YARN
The two double crochet swatches below are worked using a 4mm hook
in DK-weight wool yarn (left) and Aran-weight wool yarn (right).

The details above
show the stitches
at actual size; the
swatches on the
left are shown at
25 per cent.

CLINIC

**MY PATTERN
TALKS ABOUT
THE DRAPE. WHAT
DOES THAT MEAN?**

Drape is a description of how your
crochet fabric hangs. Is it stiff and
firm or is it light and lacy? The
characteristics of drape depend on
the stitch pattern, yarn and hook
size. A tight tension can result in a
stiff fabric, which would be ideal for
a robust project such as a crochet
bag, but less appropriate for a
shawl or wrap. Blocking your crochet
can also affect the drape – for
example, linen yarns will soften
up after washing.

It is also worth remembering that
taller stitches and stitch patterns
that have chains in them will have
more drape than a piece of fabric
worked in double crochet. The
height and the chains allow the
stitches to move more independently
of each other, creating a fabric that
moves and 'flows' more naturally.
Checking and adjusting your tension
to achieve the recommended
number of stitches and rows will
mean that your fabric will drape
in the way the designer intended,
giving a flattering fit to garments
and a sturdy, hard-wearing fabric
for bowls, bags or toys.

The tension affects the drape of the
crochet fabric as well as its overall size.

Joining yarn

You need to learn how to join in a new ball of yarn for when you run out of yarn or want to change colour. Working rows of different-coloured stripes is a simple but effective way of introducing colour and pattern into your crochet. Whenever possible, it is best to join in a new yarn at the edges of the piece of crochet for a neater result.

INCOMPLETE STITCH METHOD

Starting a new yarn is best done at the end of a row, ready to start the new yarn or colour on the first stitch of the next row. The same technique is used for working in stripes of different colours. This sequence shows changing colours in double crochet.

STEP 1
Work the last stitch of the row up to the final yarnover, then cut the yarn, leaving a 5cm (2in) tail. Lay the end of the new yarn over the hook, leaving a 5cm (2in) tail.

STEP 2
Draw the new yarn through both loops on the hook to complete the stitch. Pull the tail ends of both yarns to tighten the stitch on the hook.

STEP 3
Turn and make the turning chain using the new yarn. You can now see that by changing colours before the turning chain, the first stitch of the next row neatly begins in the new colour.

WORKING STRIPES

If you are working in stripes with an even number of rows, the colour changes will always occur at the same side of the work and so you can carry the different yarns up the side instead of cutting and rejoining them each time. This technique is known as stranding. Whenever you need to change from one colour to another, work to the final yarnover of the row, then drop the old yarn and pick up the new colour to complete the last stitch. Leave the old yarn at the side of the work until you need it for subsequent rows. If the old colour is not needed for more than two rows, wrap it around the new colour before continuing with the next row to avoid long, messy strands of yarn at the edges of your work.

WORKING OVER TAIL ENDS

When you change colours, you can leave the cut tail ends of the yarn hanging at the back of the work and weave them in with a tapestry needle after you finish your project (see page 41). With a little practice, however, it is possible to weave in the ends as you crochet along the next row by laying the tail ends behind the last row of stitches and working the next row of stitches over them. This reduces the amount of sewing at the end of your project.

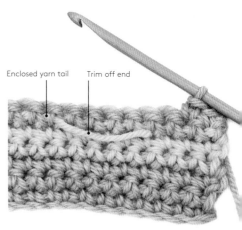

Enclosed yarn tail   Trim off end

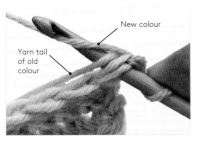

Yarn tail of old colour

New colour

STEP 1
Lay the tail ends of both the old and new yarns along the back of your work, just below the last row. If you are working in stripes, as here, and are carrying the yarns up the side of the work, there will only be one tail end when first joining in the new yarn or whenever a colour is no longer needed. Insert the hook through the first stitch of the last row and under the yarn tails, and then work the next stitch in the usual way.

Work stitches over yarn tail

STEP 2
As you complete the stitch, the yarn tails remain on the wrong side of the fabric and are enclosed within the stitch. Continue crocheting to the end of the row, working the first few stitches over the yarn tails.

STEP 3
If you turn the work over, you will see that the yarn tails are neatly secured within the stitches on the wrong side of the work. Trim the yarn tails close to the work. Try to change colours at the end of a wrong side row, so that as you work the next row, the yarn tails are woven in on the wrong side of the work.

JOINING WITH A SLIP STITCH

You can also join a new yarn using a slip stitch. This can be used with any of the basic stitches; here it is shown using treble crochet. It is best to join the new yarn at the beginning of the row.

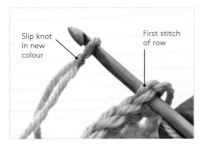

Slip knot in new colour

First stitch of row

Turning chain in new colour

STEP 1
Make a slip knot in the new yarn. Insert the hook from front to back through the first crochet stitch of the row and then pick up the slip knot.

STEP 2
Pull the slip knot through the stitch. Wrap the yarn over the hook and draw it through the slip knot to secure the yarn and make the first turning chain. Make two more turning chains (or the number required for the stitch you are working).

STEP 3
Continue working stitches using the new yarn to the end of the row. The yarn tails can be woven in afterwards or you can work the first few stitches over them (see above).

KEY

○ Chain
+ Double crochet
T Half treble crochet
T Treble crochet

CLINIC HELP! I'VE GOT A KNOT IN MY YARN. WHAT DO I DO?

Using yarn with a knot in it can create an area of weakness in your crochet. If you have enough yarn to work to the end of the row, simply follow the instructions for changing yarn in the usual way, using either the incomplete stitch method (see page 32) or the slip stitch method (see page 33). If you are in the middle of a row, work to the last yarnover of the next stitch, cut the yarn and then rejoin it after the knot using the incomplete stitch method, working over the yarn tails to the end of the row.

Uneven stripes

Worked in four colours: A, B, C and D. The last st of each row is worked into the top of the turning ch of the previous row.

Foundation chain: Using A, make any number of ch + 1.
Row 1: 1 dc in third ch from hook, 1 dc in each ch to end, turn.
Row 2: Ch 1 (counts as 1 dc), skip first st, 1 dc in each st to end, turn.
Cut A and join B.
Row 3: Ch 2 (counts as 1 htr), skip first st, 1 htr in each st to end, turn.
Row 4: As row 3.
Cut B and join C.
Row 5: Ch 3 (counts as 1 tr), skip first st, 1 tr in each st to end, turn.
Cut C and join D.
Row 6: Ch 1 (counts as 1 dc), skip first st, 1 dc in each st to end, turn.
Cut D and join C.
Row 7: Ch 2 (counts as 1 htr), skip first st, 1 htr in each st to end, turn.
Cut C and join A.
Repeats rows 2–7 for pattern using the following colour sequence:
A, B, C, D, C, B.

STRIPES WITH A DIFFERENCE

Combining different-height stitches within the row with one or more colours can be used to create a striped fabric with lots of visual interest. This is a very simple technique – really just a two-row stripe – that is often overlooked by designers in favour of the more popular chevrons (see page 98) but is well worth experimenting with.

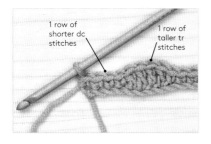

STEP 1
Working different-height stitches creates the illusion of waves. Here, four double crochet stitches are alternated with four treble crochet stitches, creating an undulating wave. A second row is then worked in the same way.

STEP 2
When you reach the point in the pattern where you need to change to a new colour to work the next stripe (here, for the third row), make a standard crochet colour change on the last yarnover (see page 32).

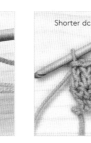

STEP 3
In this example, the third row of the pattern is still composed of alternating stitches, but this time the shorter double crochet are worked over the treble crochet of previous rows, and vice versa.

Undulating stripes

Worked in two colours, A and B. The colour changes every two rows. Do not cut the yarn after each colour change; carry the unused yarn up the side of the work. The last st of each row is worked into the top of the turning ch of the previous row.

Foundation chain: Using A, make a multiple of 8 ch + 5.
Row 1: 1 dc in third ch from hook, 1 dc in each of next 2 ch, *1 tr in each of next 4 ch, 1 dc in each of next 4 ch; rep from * to end, turn.
Row 2: Ch 1 (counts as 1 dc), skip first st, 1 dc in each of next 3 sts, *1 tr in each of next 4 sts, 1 dc in each of next 4 sts; rep from * to end, changing to B on final yo, turn.
Row 3: Ch 3 (counts as 1 tr), skip first st, 1 tr in each of next 3 sts, *1 dc in each of next 4 sts, 1 tr in each of next 4 sts; rep from * to end, turn.

Row 4: Ch 3 (counts as 1 tr), skip first st, 1 tr in each of next 3 sts, *1 dc in each of next 4 sts, 1 tr in each of next 4 sts; rep from * to end, changing to A on final yo, turn.
Row 5: Ch 1 (counts as 1 dc), skip first st, 1 dc in each of next 3 sts, *1 tr in each of next 4 sts, 1 dc in each of next 4 sts; rep from * to end, turn.
Row 6: As row 2.
Repeat rows 3–6 for pattern.

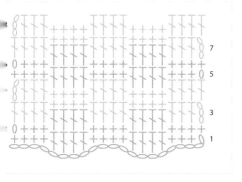

KEY
⌒ Chain
+ Double crochet
T Treble crochet

Shaping

Shaping refers to the process of increasing or decreasing the number of stitches. Being able to create different shapes opens up new opportunities for crocheting toys or making garments. Both increases and decreases can be worked anywhere along a row for gradual shaping, or you can add or subtract multiple stitches at the edges of the crochet fabric to create stepped shaping. The swatches below demonstrate the shaping techniques explained on the following pages.

CLINIC : MY EDGES LOOK MESSY WHERE I'VE WORKED AN INTERNAL INCREASE. HOW CAN I MAKE THEM NEATER?

To make a neat edge at the start of a row, work the first stitch and then work the increase. At the end of the row, work until two stitches remain (the last stitch will probably be the turning chain from the previous row). Work the increase into the next to last stitch, then work the last stitch as usual. Internal increases are often used at the beginning and end of rows to shape garment edges, so using this method will make the edges straighter for sewing into a seam later.

MITRED SQUARE
Starting from a foundation chain equal to the length of two adjacent sides of the square, a double internal decrease is worked at the centre of each row to create a mitred square shape.

DIAMOND
Internal increases are worked on each side up to the halfway point, and then internal decreases on each side up to the top point.

CHEVRON
An internal increase and decrease at each edge shape the bottom half of the chevron, then the same technique is used but in the opposite direction to complete the top half.

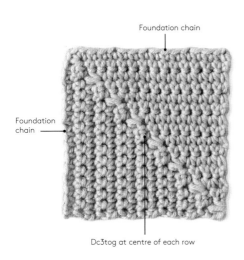

Foundation chain

Foundation chain

Dc3tog at centre of each row

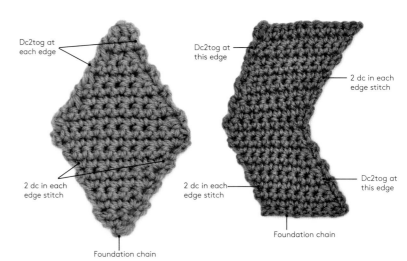

Dc2tog at each edge

2 dc in each edge stitch

Foundation chain

Dc2tog at this edge

2 dc in each edge stitch

2 dc in each edge stitch

Dc2tog at this edge

Foundation chain

T SHAPE
External increases are worked at each side to increase the width of the fabric at the top.

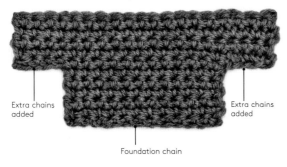

Extra chains added

Extra chains added

Foundation chain

INVERTED T SHAPE
External decreases are worked at each side to reduce the width of the fabric at the top.

Work turned before end of row

Slip stitches worked at beginning of row

Foundation chain

INCREASING

The most common way to increase is to work two (or more) stitches into the same place. This method is useful for adding stitches anywhere across a row, and is known as an internal increase. You can also create extra stitches at either end of a row by adding extra chains and working into them; this is called an external or stepped increase. The examples shown here are worked in double crochet, but the technique is the same for all the basic stitches.

INTERNAL INCREASE

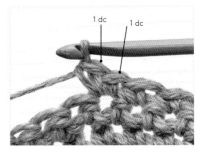

STEP 1
Work to the point where you want to increase, then work a double crochet into the next stitch on the previous row in the usual way.

STEP 2
Instead of moving on to the following stitch on the previous row, work a second double crochet into the same stitch.

STEP 3
You have now increased by one stitch, known as a single increase. You can increase by more than one stitch at a time by working more stitches into the same stitch on the previous row – for example, work a third double crochet in the same place to increase by two stitches, known as a double increase.

EXTERNAL INCREASE

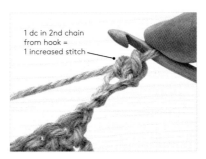

STEP 1
To add multiple stitches at the edge of the crochet, work to the end of the previous row and then make the number of chains needed for the turning chain plus one extra chain for each extra stitch you wish to increase by. In this double crochet example, we are increasing by three stitches, so four chains have been made – one turning chain plus three extra chains for the increase. For taller stitches, remember that you will need to work more turning chains.

STEP 2
Skip the turning chain (in this example one chain stitch) and then work a double crochet stitch into each of the extra chains in the same way as when working into the foundation chain.

STEP 3
Three extra stitches have been created. Count the stitches before continuing to make sure that you have the new number of stitches stated in the pattern.

STEP 4
To make symmetrical increases at each side of the work – known as paired increases – make extra chains at the end of two consecutive rows.

DECREASING

Reducing the number of stitches is known as decreasing. This can be used to create shapes and effects such as chevrons, or for creating armholes or necklines on garments. Sometimes a complex stitch pattern is created by pairing a series of increases and decreases across a row.

INTERNAL DECREASE USING DOUBLE CROCHET

This method makes it easy to reduce stitches evenly across a row. The most common is a single decrease, made by working two stitches together in order to decrease by one stitch. The abbreviation for decreasing one stitch in double crochet is 'dc2tog', which means double crochet two together. It is possible to decrease more than two stitches at a time following the same principle. A decrease of two stitches, for example, known as a double decrease, is made by working three stitches together. In double crochet, this is abbreviated to 'dc3tog'.

First incomplete dc

STEP 1
Follow the pattern up to the position of the decrease, then work the next double crochet stitch as far as the last yarnover; you will have two loops on the hook.

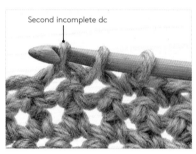

Second incomplete dc

STEP 2
Insert the hook into the next stitch and draw the yarn through, so that you have three loops on the hook.

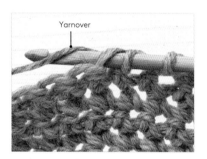

Yarnover

STEP 3
Wrap the yarn over the hook and draw it through all three loops on the hook.

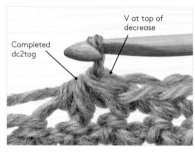

V at top of decrease

Completed dc2tog

STEP 4
The finished decrease will look like this, with two double crochet stitches joined together at the top. There will be a single V-shaped loop on top of the decrease. On the next row, treat the decrease as a single stitch and work under both loops of the V in the usual way.

3 DECREASES WITH A TWIST

1 You can decrease by skipping (or missing) a stitch. This technique is sometimes used at the beginning of a row, but it can leave a gap. Beginners often make this decrease by accident and it is a common reason why your crochet might not be straight – another reason to get into the habit of regularly counting your stitches.

2 With thicker yarns, the conventional decrease of working multiple stitches together (for example, dc2tog) can leave a hole or gap in your work. To avoid this, don't insert the hook under both loops of the V at the top of the stitches on the previous row as you normally would. Instead, work the first stitch into the front loop only of the first stitch, and then work the second stitch into the back loop only of the next stitch. This can give a neater finish and make your work look more professional. (See page 77 for a similar decrease method known as an invisible decrease that is popular with amigurumi.)

3 Simply turn your work at the end of the row without working the last stitch. This leaves a slight step in your work and is used less often than working two stitches together.

STEPPED EDGE
The right edge of this swatch was shaped by turning the work before the end of the row (see 3, above). Note the stepped edge this creates.

INTERNAL DECREASE USING OTHER STITCHES

You can work internal decreases with the other basic crochet stitches using the same principle as double crochet. Start by working the first stitch but stop before the last yarnover, leaving the stitch incomplete. Then work the second stitch in the usual way, but when you work the final yarnover, draw the yarn through all the loops on the hook to join them together. Here, two treble crochet are being worked together, which is abbreviated to 'tr2tog' in patterns.

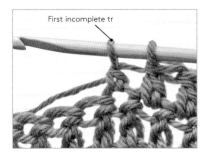

First incomplete tr

Second incomplete tr

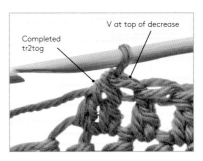

V at top of decrease

Completed tr2tog

STEP 1
Work up to the place where you want to decrease. Wrap the yarn over the hook and insert the hook into the stitch. Catch the yarn and draw it through the stitch (three loops on hook). Wrap the yarn over the hook and draw it through the first two loops (two loops on hook). Stop working the first treble at this point, leaving the stitch incomplete.

STEP 2
Wrap the yarn over the hook, insert the hook into the next stitch and work the second treble crochet until you have three loops on the hook.

STEP 3
Wrap the yarn over the hook and draw it through all three loops to complete the decrease. The finished decrease will look like this, with two treble crochet stitches joined together at the top, and a single V-shaped loop on top of the decrease. On the next row, treat the decrease as a single stitch and work under both loops of the V in the usual way.

EXTERNAL DECREASE

External decreases are used to subtract groups of stitches at the beginning and end of rows. This a common method for creating armhole shaping on simple garments. The technique can be used with any of the basic crochet stitches.

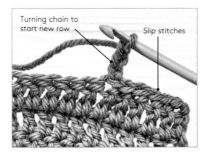

Turning chain to start new row

Slip stitches

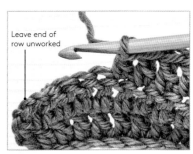

Leave end of row unworked

STEP 1
At the beginning of a row, a pattern may tell you to decrease by working slip stitch across a certain number of stitches. You should then work the appropriate turning chain and continue along the row in the required stitch pattern. On subsequent rows, the slipped stitches are left unworked. At first, you may find it helpful to insert a stitch marker into the last slip stitch so that you do not work into it accidentally on the next row.

STEP 2
To decrease at the end of a row, simply turn the work before reaching the end of the row. Your pattern will instruct you when to turn. The remaining stitches are simply ignored on subsequent rows.

Finishing

Spending time learning to finish your work neatly can make all the difference to your crochet project. This section covers the most common and useful techniques to give your work a professional finish: weaving in any loose yarn ends; blocking or pressing your work to even out the stitches and set the shape; and joining pieces of crochet together with sewn or crocheted seams.

WEAVING IN ENDS

Every project has at least two ends of yarn, one at the beginning and one at the end, and these need to be woven in and secured on the wrong side of the fabric. Always leave generous yarn tails – about 10–15cm (4–6in) – so that you have enough yarn to thread on to a tapestry needle for weaving in. There is no right or wrong way to weave in ends, and every crocheter has their own preferred method – across the back of stitches, up and down them or even diagonally. Be aware that some fibres, such as cotton and silk, can be a little slippery and work loose, so you need to make sure they are secured. Others, such as wool and mohair, cling to each other and are less likely to work loose. A contrasting colour is used here for clarity.

ACROSS A ROW
Weave the yarn through the back of several stitches across the row on the wrong side of the crochet, then trim the remaining end. Take care that the yarn does not show through on the other side.

ALONG ROW ENDS

STEP 1
For taller stitches, such as treble crochet, it can be easier to weave the yarn up and down the back of the stitches. Start by weaving the tail down the row ends.

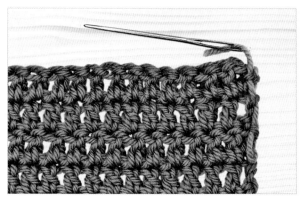

STEP 2
Turn the needle and go upwards to secure the yarn tail, then trim the remaining end.

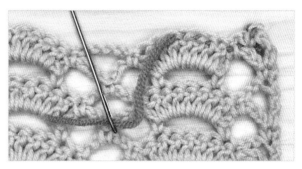

WEAVING IN MORE THAN ONE COLOUR

If you have used more than one colour of yarn, weave in all the yarn ends separately behind stitches of the same colour. Try to space them slightly so that not all yarn tails are woven through the same stitches. Trim the remaining ends neatly when you have finished.

WEAVING IN ON LACY PATTERNS

For openwork or lace patterns, you can weave the yarn end through the yarnovers of taller stitches or through the back of chains. Place the needle where the woven ends will be least conspicuous on the right side of the fabric. If you will be sewing a seam, make sure to weave in the yarn ends slightly away from the edge to avoid bulk in the seam.

PRESSING

You can improve the appearance of your finished crochet by pressing or blocking (see page 42). These techniques are used to even out uneven stitches and set the shape of the crochet fabric. Sometimes all that your work needs is a light press with a cool iron to flatten it out or neaten the edges before sewing them together. Refer to the instructions on the yarn's ball band. Some recommend pressing under a dry cloth, others under a damp cloth for steam. If in doubt about the suitability of pressing, use your tension swatch as a test piece. Use a light touch when pressing, to avoid crushing the stitches. Always lift and replace the iron on to the cloth, rather than moving the iron around on the surface.

CLINIC HOW DO I KNOW WHETHER TO BLOCK OR PRESS MY CROCHET?

It is largely a matter of personal preference, but here are some guidelines:
- Pieces that are to be sewn together will always benefit from blocking (see page 42) or pressing (see left).
- Some items, such as amigurumi, toys or novelty items, do not need to be blocked or pressed and can be used as soon as they are finished.
- Blocking is preferable for boldly textured stitch patterns and for projects that include several different yarn fibres.
- You can press any yarns labelled on the ball band with a recommended ironing temperature (usually natural fibres, such as wool or cotton).
- Any yarns labelled 'do not press' (such as synthetic and textured yarns) must be blocked rather than pressed.

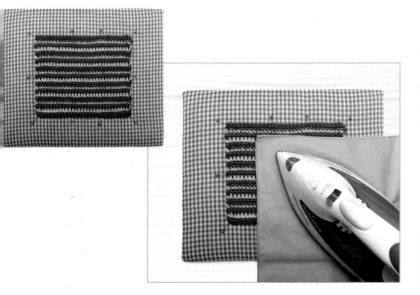

BLOCKING

Many beginners are put off by this term, not understanding what it means and often ignoring it completely, but it can make all the difference to your final piece of crochet. Blocking involves easing and pinning the crochet fabric into the correct shape. It usually involves water or steam, which allows the fibres in the yarn to reveal their true qualities. It is also a useful way to flatten any pieces that may be curling, and to neaten the edges before sewing them together. You will need a flat surface to work on, some towels or absorbent material (make sure they are colourfast) and some pins. The blocking method you use is largely a matter of personal choice.

WET BLOCKING

Most commonly used for natural fibres, wet blocking takes a little more time, but it can completely transform your project. If you have used a pale-coloured yarn, wet blocking is also an opportunity to make sure the crochet is clean and blemish-free.

STEP 1
Soak the crochet fabric in cold or tepid water for at least 10 minutes (check the ball band to see what is recommended). You can use a mild soap or a proprietary wool wash.

STEP 2
Drain off the water and gently squeeze out the excess water. Don't wring it out or stretch it because the fibres are very fragile when wet. It may be helpful to wrap the crochet in a towel to help you get rid of excess water.

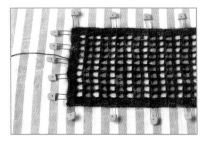

STEP 3
Once you have squeezed out the excess water, lay the work on a flat surface. Gently pin it out to the correct shape or dimensions given in the pattern and allow to dry completely before unpinning.

STEAM BLOCKING

If you don't have time to wet block or your items are small, then steam blocking can help. Lay the crochet on a flat surface or ironing board and pin it to shape. Hold a warm iron over the crochet, making sure it does not touch the fibres. Apply gentle steam over the whole piece and allow it to dry completely. Useful for natural or synthetic yarns, it is important to remember that direct heat can destroy woollen fibres and melt acrylic, so use caution and take your time when using this method.

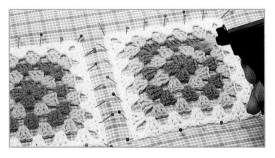

COLD BLOCKING

Pin the work out on to a flat surface, placing towels underneath to absorb any water. Following any dimensions or instructions in the pattern, gently pull the crochet fabric into shape and use pins to make sure it stays in place. Fill a spray bottle with cold or tepid water and spray liberally over the crochet. Allow to dry completely before unpinning. This is usually all a project made using synthetic fibres will need.

STITCHED SEAMS

Crochet pieces can be stitched together using a tapestry needle. As a general rule, use the same yarn as the project for sewing seams (but see also clinic on page 44). For multicolour pieces, choose a colour that blends in as much as possible. Use pins to hold the pieces together while you stitch. A contrasting colour is used here for clarity.

BACKSTITCH

Backstitch creates an invisible seam that is secure and inelastic, because each stitch overlaps the previous one. It is very useful for joining seams on a garment or for bags, homewares and items that need to stand up to regular use.

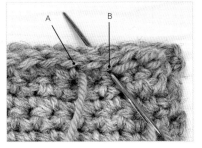

STEP 1
Place the pieces to be joined right sides together and hold in place with pins. Make sure that you align the edges of each piece so that stitches and rows line up neatly.

STEP 2
Starting at the right edge of the work, secure the yarn with one or two stitches. Work a row of backstitches from right to left, close to the edge. For each stitch, bring the needle through to the front a short distance farther along from the previous stitch (A), then take it through to the back where the previous stitch ends (B).

STEP 3
Repeat this across the edge to join the two pieces. Make sure you fasten off the yarn securely so that the seam does not unravel.

WHIP STITCH

Sometimes called oversewing or overcast stitch, this is more flexible than backstitch. It is very useful around armholes, where the fabric needs to be secure but flexible. It is very popular with crochet designers and experienced crocheters because it creates an almost invisible seam. If you use a contrasting colour yarn, it can provide a decorative finish on the right side of the fabric.

STEP 1
Pin the pieces to be joined together, as for backstitch. Working from right to left, take the needle over the edge of the work and then bring it from back to front through both layers of fabric. Sew across the pieces to be joined from right to left, making each stitch slightly in front of the previous stitch.

STEP 2
When working along the top of rows, as here, insert the needle under the V shape at the top of the stitches. When working along row edges, make sure to sew through the stitch or turning chain and not into the gaps between stitches to give your work a neater and more stable finish.

CROCHETED SEAMS

Crocheting seams together is a popular method of joining for accessories, blankets and items that need a strong, secure seam. Crochet seams are less popular for garments because the finished seam is more bulky than a sewn seam. A crochet seam can be worked on the right side of the fabric to embellish your work. When you crochet a seam, work into the stitches rather than the gaps between stitches for a neater and more secure finish. A contrasting colour is used here for clarity.

SLIP STITCH SEAM

This makes a strong seam without flexibility. Use it for sewing seams on bags, cushion covers and other items that will receive a lot of wear and tear. Place the pieces to be joined right sides together and secure them with pins before you start.

STEP 1

With the yarn at the back of the work, insert the hook through both layers of fabric at the right edge. If you are joining a top or bottom edge, as here, insert the hook under the V at the top of each stitch. On side seams, work the slip stitches one stitch in from the edge to create a neat and stable seam.

Insert hook under Vs at top of stitches

Loop 1

Insert hook under next pair of Vs

STEP 2
Draw a loop of yarn through both layers.

STEP 3
Insert the hook from front to back through the next pair of stitches.

Loop 2

Pull loop 2 through loop 1 to complete slip stitch

STEP 4
Catch the yarn at the back of the work and draw a loop through to the front.

STEP 5
Draw the second loop through the first loop to make the first slip stitch join.

STEP 6
Continue in this way until the fabric seam is completed. Fasten off the yarn and weave in the ends.

CLINIC : HOW DO I KNOW WHICH SEAMING METHOD IS BEST FOR MY PROJECT?

There are several ways to join the pieces of your finished crochet project together. The method you use depends on what you are seaming and personal choice. The most common stitched and crocheted seams are described here, with advice on when to use them, but these are only guidelines.

Whichever method you choose, make sure that each stitch is a similar size. Do not pull the stitches too tightly or they will pucker. After spending many hours on a crochet project, the extra time spent finishing your work is worth the effort to make it look polished and tidy. It is often said that a well-finished project elevates it from homemade to handmade. The skills needed to seam proficiently may take a little practice, so use your test swatches to try out the techniques and you will find that your confidence and skill will grow.

CONCEALED DOUBLE CROCHET SEAM

Joining a seam with double crochet gives a firm but flexible finish, and is useful for joining seams on garments. Before you start, place the pieces to be joined right sides together and hold in place with pins.

Work a row of dc

STEP 1
Holding the yarn behind the work, insert the hook through both layers of fabric and work a row of double crochet close to the edge of the fabric. Space the stitches evenly to keep the seam flat and prevent puckering. If you are joining the top or bottom of a crochet piece, use the top V of each stitch as a guide, making one double crochet in each stitch as you work across.

STEP 2
On the reverse, you can see a neat row of stitches that will be almost invisible when worked in the same colour as the fabric.

DECORATIVE DOUBLE CROCHET SEAM

Work as for the concealed seam, but with wrong sides together. This is a useful technique for blankets and homewares, or for garments that require a decorative edging. As the finished seam does not lie flat, it is generally used on the edges of items such as cushion covers, or for joining motifs where the raised edge is used to add texture to the crochet.

1 Make sure that the rows and stitches of the pieces being joined together are aligned before you begin seaming. Using pins helps to keep the crochet fabric in place.

2 Use the same hook to crochet seams as you used for the project.

3 For best results, work one joining stitch into each crochet stitch along the row. When working down the side edges, you may need to make more joining stitches, depending on the height of the crochet stitch – for example, if the fabric has been made using treble crochet, you may need more joining stitches for each row. Generally three stitches for every two trebles is recommended, but you will need to judge this yourself by eye or follow the instructions in the pattern.

4 After seaming, you may need to press the fabric. Open out the seam and press lightly on the reverse with a warm iron to flatten it (check the ball band to make sure the yarn is suitable, or place a cotton cloth on top of the crochet to protect it from the heat of the iron).

5 Take your time. Neat, professional-looking seams make all the difference to the appearance of your finished crochet. Working in good light on a flat surface is essential.

1 dc being worked

Ch 1

DOUBLE CROCHET AND CHAIN SEAM

Pin the pieces to be joined with right sides together, placing the pins at right angles to the edge. With the yarn at the back, insert the hook through both layers of fabric and work a double crochet stitch to begin the seam. Make one chain, then work another double crochet a short distance from the first. Repeat the sequence of 1 dc, ch 1 along the edge of the fabric, placing the stitches evenly to ensure the seam lies flat and the fabric does not pucker.

Quick start project:

Fingerless gloves

With no shaping and using just double crochet stitches, these fingerless gloves are an ideal first project for a beginner. The simple stripe detail adds a touch of colour and pattern interest.

FINISHED SIZE
Circumference (will stretch):
Small: 17cm (6³⁄₄in)
Medium: 19cm (7¹⁄₂in)
Large: 21cm (8¹⁄₄in)
Length (all sizes):
18cm (7in)

TENSION
16 sts and 22 rows = 10cm (4in) square over double crochet

YOU WILL NEED
• 1 x 50g ball of DK-weight wool yarn in each of yellow (A), dark blue (B) and light blue (C); Tracey used DMC Woolly, 100% merino wool with approx. 125m (136yd) per ball, in 092 (A), 077 (B) and 071 (C), but any DK yarn can be substituted
• 4mm crochet hook
• Yarn needle

ABBREVIATIONS AND TECHNIQUES
ch = chain (page 18)
dc = double crochet (page 23)
RS = right side
st(s) = stitch(es)
Joining yarn (page 32)
Backstitch (page 43)

PATTERN NOTES
• The instructions are for three sizes, with the smallest size given first followed by the two larger sizes in parentheses – small(medium:large). The pattern begins at the cuff.
• Ch 1 at the beginning of each row does not count as a stitch.
• Adjust the length of the gloves by working more or fewer rows in yarn A.
• You can use either the incomplete stitch method or the slip stitch method for joining the different yarn colours. When changing colours, do not cut the yarn unless indicated in the pattern; carry unused yarn up the side of the work between stripes.

GLOVES (MAKE 2)
Foundation chain: Using B, ch 27(29:31).
Row 1: 1 dc in second ch from hook, 1 dc in each ch to end, turn. (26[28:30] sts)
Row 2: Ch 1, 1 dc in each st to end, turn.
Continue to work in double crochet for 25 rows in the following colour sequence:
Rows 3–4: Yarn C.
Rows 5–6: Yarn B.
Rows 7–8: Yarn C.
Rows 9–10: Yarn B.
Cut yarns B and C.
Rows 11–36: Yarn A.
Cut yarn A and then work the following two rows in double crochet.
Rows 37–38: Yarn B.
Fasten off and weave in ends.
With RS together, fold each glove in half and sew side seam using backstitch, leaving a gap for thumb.
Turn RS out.

Quick start project:

Bunting

Bunting always evokes a party atmosphere and is perfect for adding colour to a playroom or for hanging outdoors for a summer celebration. The simple decreasing and double crochet stitch make this an easy project for a beginner.

FINISHED SIZE
Each triangle: 15 x 11cm (6 x 4¼in) at widest and longest points
Length: approx. 230cm (90in)

TENSION
Make the first triangle and check against stated dimensions; if necessary, adjust size of hook if you want to match stated size

YOU WILL NEED
• 1 x 50g ball of DK-weight wool yarn in each of four bright colours plus white; Tracey used DMC Woolly, 100% merino wool with approx. 125m (136yd) per ball, in 061, 074, 084, 102 and 03, but any DK yarn can be substituted
• 4mm crochet hook
• Yarn needle

ABBREVIATIONS AND TECHNIQUES
ch = chain (page 18)
dc = double crochet (page 23)
dc2tog/dc3tog = double crochet 2/3 together
rep = repeat
st(s) = stitch(es)
Internal decreases (page 38)

PATTERN NOTES
• The triangles are worked from the top edge down to the point.
• Ch 1 at the beginning of each row does not count as a stitch.
• You can vary the length of the bunting by adding more triangles and varying the space between joining each triangle.

TRIANGLES (MAKE 12)
Make three triangles in each of four bright colours.
Foundation chain: Ch 22.
Row 1: 1 dc in second ch from hook, 1 dc in each ch to end, turn. (21 sts)
Row 2: Ch 1, dc2tog, 1 dc in each st to last 2 sts, dc2tog, turn. (19 sts)
Row 3: Ch 1, 1 dc in each st to end, turn.
Rows 4–18: Repeat rows 2–3 until 3 sts remain, ending with a row 2.
Row 19: Dc3tog.
Fasten off.

EDGING (EACH TRIANGLE)
Rejoin yarn to top left corner of triangle, work 3 dc in corner, then work 1 dc in each row end down to base, 3 dc in bottom point, 1 dc in each row end up to top right corner, 3 dc in corner, 1 dc in each st to end of round.
Fasten off and weave in ends.
Press each triangle lightly to flatten before making up.

ASSEMBLING THE BUNTING
Row 1: Using white yarn, ch 30, *pick up triangle and work 1 dc in each st along top edge, ch 4; rep from * until all triangles have been joined, arranging colours in sequence. After joining last triangle, ch 30, turn.
Row 2: Ch 1, 1 dc in each dc and ch to end.
Fasten off.
Hanging loops: Using white yarn, ch 10. Cut yarn and tie yarn tails together with a knot. Make second loop in same way and sew to either end of bunting using the yarn tails.

Guest Designer Ali Campbell

I live in rural north Dorset in the UK and have found my niche in the wonderful world of crochet. As well as creating my own crochet designs, I also teach others how to crochet, both in a classroom in my own home – the aptly named 'Old School' – and at local venues in the nearby towns of Shaftesbury and Sherborne. I hope to expand my teaching in the coming years as my passion is to pass on this amazing, flexible craft to others. I have written my own self-published book, *Crochet for Beginners who want to Improve*, and am planning book number 2 soon. You can find out more about me and my work at www.gethookedoncrochet.co.uk.

Soft scarf with nubby tassels

This scarf is easy to make, using some of the basic stitches you have learned in this chapter. It will grow quickly in this luxuriously chunky wool.

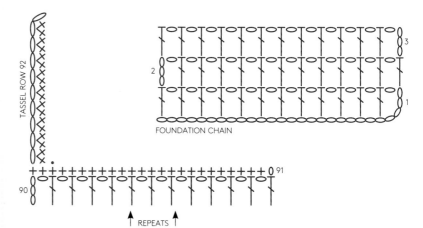

FINISHED SIZE
18 x 92cm (7 x 36in)

TENSION
18 sts (counting each tr and each ch as 1 st) and 4 rows = 10cm (4in) square over pattern after blocking

YOU WILL NEED
- 5 x 50g balls of chunky-weight wool yarn; Ali chose Bergere de France Merinos Alpaga, 60% merino wool/40% alpaca with approx. 65m (71yd) per ball, in Bleu Ciel 29905
- 7mm crochet hook
- Yarn needle

ABBREVIATIONS AND TECHNIQUES
beg = beginning
ch = chain (page 18)
dc = double crochet (page 23)
rep = repeat
sl st = slip stitch (page 22)
st(s) = stitch(es)
tr = treble crochet (page 24)
Crochet cords (page 120)

PATTERN NOTES
- Ch 4 at the beginning of a row counts as 1 tr and ch 1.
- The tassels are spiral cords worked on to each end of the scarf.

SCARF
Foundation chain: Ch 28.
Row 1: 1 tr in sixth ch from hook, ch 1, *skip next ch, 1 tr in next ch, ch 1; rep from * ending 1 tr in last ch, turn. (13 tr)
Rows 2–90: Ch 4, skip first tr, *1 tr in next st, ch 1; rep from * ending 1 tr in 3rd ch of beg ch-4, turn.

TASSELS
Row 91: Ch 1 (counts as 1 dc), 1 dc in each st and ch across, ending 1 dc in 3rd ch of beg ch-4, turn. (25 sts)
Row 92: *Ch 10, 2 dc in 2nd ch from hook and in each ch to end, skip next st on row 91, sl st in next st; rep from * ending sl st in ch-1 of row 91. (13 tassels)
Fasten off and weave in ends.
Join yarn to foundation chain at other end of scarf and repeat rows 91–92 once more.
Fasten off and weave in ends.

KEY
◯ Chain
• Slip stitch
+ Double crochet
T Treble crochet
XX 2 dc in same place

TASSEL ROW 92

FOUNDATION CHAIN

REPEATS

Be inspired

1. BERTIE BABY BLANKET, AMY ASTLE
Different-height stitches (dc, htr, tr) and a colour palette of brights on a neutral background have been used to create this eye-catching blanket. An edging in a neutral colour allows any yarn tails to be disguised and adds a professional finish.

2. MAISY ROPER BAG, TRACEY TODHUNTER
Chunky alpaca yarn and leather accessories, such as the strap and buckle, turns a simple double crochet bag into a stylish fashion piece. The fabric has been crocheted on a smaller hook, creating a stiff and durable fabric.

3. KNOTTED HEADBAND, STEPHANIE LAU
Two strips of treble crochet have been transformed into a wearable accessory. Wrapping a shorter, narrower piece of crochet around a simple headband adds visual interest and a flattering shape. The gathers created by wrapping the shorter piece to create the illusion of a knot is a creative way to add shape without tackling increasing and decreasing.

4. FINGERLESS GLOVES,
TRACEY TODHUNTER
A bright colour and wooden buttons are used to turn the simplest piece of double crochet into a stylish accessory. A crochet buttonhole makes the thumb slit, and buttons have been sewn along the side seam.

5. CROCHET HANDBAG,
RASA GRIGAITE
This pretty bag shows how bold colours and simple textures can be used to

great effect. Adding wooden handles and a ribbon trim turns this double crochet project into a fashion piece. The gathered top edge has been created by threading ribbon through a row of treble crochet.

6. STUFFED HEART,
LEONIE MORGAN
Two crochet motifs have been joined together with a decorative slip stitch seam and stuffed to create a simple ornament. The heart shape is made

using a combination of different-height stitches and a simple chain has been used to make a hanging loop.

7. LARGE COWL, STEPHANIE LAU
Tall, open stitches have been used to create a stunning accessory. The long strip has been joined along the short sides to create a tube. The designer has cleverly used a bold colour to add visual impact.

CHAPTER 2
Working in the Round

Working in rounds rather than back and forth in rows is the basis for many crochet projects, and allows you to create all kinds of shapes, from simple circular motifs to three-dimensional tubes for amigurumi (a technique for making small toys and mascots). The quick start projects give you the opportunity to put your new skills into practice, and the chapter concludes with a simple toy to make.

Starting the round

Working in the round always begins with a centre ring. The crochet stitches are worked into the ring and progressively outwards from there. The three most common types of ring are a foundation ring of chains, a magic ring and a finger wrap. When completed, the three techniques look very similar. If a pattern does not specify which to use, choose the one you prefer. The aim is to create a secure ring that will not work loose over time.

FOUNDATION RING

This is simply a foundation chain that is joined together at the ends with a slip stitch to form a ring. The ring needs to be big enough to work the first round of stitches into, and the pattern will tell you how many chains to make. This is the most secure and robust of all the rings.

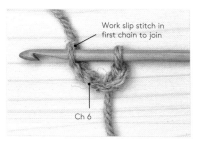

STEP 1
Make the required number of chains (six are used here), then join into a ring by working a slip stitch into the first chain.

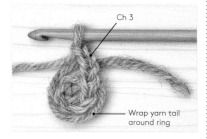

STEP 2
If you wish, wrap the yarn tail around the chain ring so that you can enclose the tail as you work. You are now ready to make the first round of stitches. For a round of treble crochet, as here, make three chains for the starting chain; this counts as the first stitch of the round.

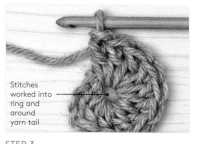

STEP 3
Work the required number of stitches into the ring, enclosing the yarn tail in the stitches as you go. Note that the stitches should be worked into the centre of the ring, not into the chains.

STEP 4
Make a slip stitch into the top chain of the starting chain to join the round and complete the circle.

MAGIC RING

The adjustable or magic ring has become a popular way to start crochet in rounds, especially in amigurumi patterns. The technique avoids the hole that often occurs at the centre of a traditional foundation ring.

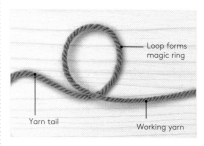

STEP 1
Loop the yarn around to form a ring.

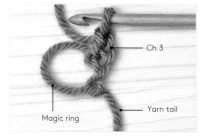

STEP 2
Insert the hook through the centre of the ring and draw through a loop of the working yarn (the yarn coming from the ball). Work the required number of starting chains (here, three chains).

The round may begin with a number of chains to bring the hook up to the correct height for the stitch you will be working next. This is the same as the turning chain when working in rows, but is known as a starting chain when working in rounds. Just as with rows, the starting chain may count as the first stitch; the pattern will tell you if this is the case.

FINGER WRAP

A less common but useful technique for making a ring is the finger wrap. The yarn tail forms part of the finger wrap and is enclosed within the first few stitches to make a secure ring. This technique works best with woollen yarns; more slippery fibres such as silk and cotton may work loose over time.

STEP 1
Wind the yarn two or three times around one or two fingers.

STEP 2
Slip the yarn off your fingers, insert the hook into the ring and pull a loop of the working yarn through the centre.

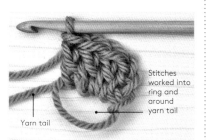

STEP 3
Work the required number of crochet stitches, working them into the centre of the ring and over the yarn tail as you make each stitch (it is important to work over the yarn tail with a magic ring).

STEP 3
Make a chain to secure the yarn ring before working the starting chain.

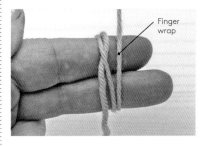

STEP 4
Work the required number of starting chains and stitches into the ring, working over the yarn tail as you make each stitch.

STEP 4
After making the last stitch, gently pull the yarn tail to close the hole at the centre. Work a slip stitch into the top of the starting chain to close the round.

STEP 5
Gently pull the yarn tail to close the hole. Join the round by working a slip stitch into the top of the starting chain.

Circles and spirals

Circular shapes are made by working regular increases on each round. It is the evenly spaced increases that help to create the shape and keep it flat. If you stop increasing, your crochet will grow into a tube (see page 70). The first and last stitches of each round are joined with a slip stitch when crocheting circles. Spirals are not joined, and each round is worked without a starting chain to create a spiral effect.

MAKING A CIRCLE

You can make a circle using any crochet stitch. This example begins with a foundation ring (see page 56) and is worked using treble crochet for each round. Each round begins with three chains for the starting chain, which counts as the first treble crochet stitch.

CLINIC : HOW MANY INCREASES SHOULD I MAKE?

The height of the stitch and the stitch pattern you are working will determine how many increases you need to make on each round. The taller the stitch, the more increases required to create a flat, regular shape. Too few increases and the shape will pucker or curl; too many and the edges will become uneven and frilly. Always count your stitches before beginning the next round to ensure you have made the correct number of increases. The pattern will always tell you how many increases to make and where to space them.

STEP 1
Work the first round into the foundation ring (here, 12 tr) and then make a slip stitch into the top of the starting chain to join the round into a circle. You may find it helpful to place a marker in the top of the last stitch to help you identify the end of the round. Move the marker into the last stitch of each new round as you progress.

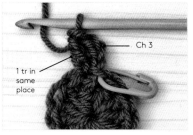

STEP 2
Work the starting chain and then work one treble crochet stitch into the same place as the starting chain (written as 'ch 3, 1 tr in same place' in a pattern). By working the treble crochet into the same place as the starting chain, you have made two stitches in the same place, thereby increasing by one stitch.

STEP 3
Continue increasing by working two trebles into each stitch of the previous round, then join the round with a slip stitch as before. Move the marker. This completes the second round of the circle (24 tr in total).

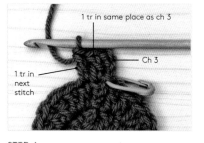

STEP 4
Start the third round by working ch 3, 1 tr in the same place as the slip stitch join, followed by 1 tr in the next stitch.

STEP 5
Work 2 tr in the next stitch and then 1 tr in the following stitch. Repeat this sequence to the end of the round and then join with a slip stitch. Count the stitches; you should now have 36 trebles. You can use the same principle of working increases evenly on each round to increase the size of the circle.

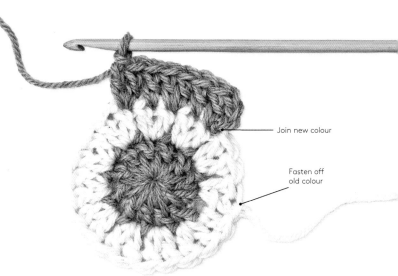

CHANGING COLOURS

You can work each round of your circle in a different colour. The simplest way is to change colour on the last yarnover using the incomplete stitch method, just as when working in rows (see page 32). However, you will get a neater result if you fasten off the first colour at the end of the round, then join the new colour with a slip stitch (see page 33) to a different part of the circle to work the next round.

Join new colour

Fasten off old colour

NEATER JOINING

When joining rounds, the usual method is to join the first and last stitches together with a slip stitch. This method works very well, but sometimes leaves a small gap. As you grow in confidence, you may wish to try this method to create an invisible join. This technique is sometimes called grafting the stitch. It requires you to cut and rejoin the yarn on every round, which is not a problem if you are working each round in a different colour, but can result in lots of extra ends to weave in if you are working in a single colour. Some crocheters use this method to join the final round only.

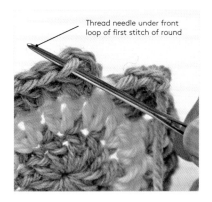

Thread needle under front loop of first stitch of round

STEP 1
Work to the last stitch of the round, but do not join with a slip stitch. Fasten off the yarn, leaving a 15cm (6in) tail. Thread the yarn tail on to a tapestry needle. Insert the needle from front to back under the front loop of the first stitch at the beginning of the round and draw the yarn through (be careful to locate the first stitch, not the starting chain).

Back loop of last stitch of round

Pull yarn tail through

STEP 2
Insert the needle from front to back under the back loop of the last stitch of the round and draw the yarn through.

STEP 3
Adjust the tension of the sewn stitch so that the circle lies flat, then weave in the ends on the reverse.

Grafted joins

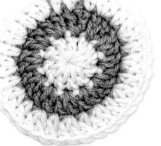

Slip stitch joins

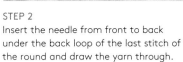

Sun in the centre

Foundation ring: Ch 6 and join with sl st to form a ring.
Round 1: Ch 1 (counts as 1 dc), 9 dc into ring, join with sl st to first dc. (10 dc)
Round 2: Ch 5 (counts as 1 tr, ch 2), [1 tr in next dc, ch 2] 9 times, join with sl st to 3rd ch of beg ch-5. (10 tr)
Round 3: Ch 3 (counts as 1 tr) [2 tr in next ch-2 sp, 1 tr in next tr] 9 times, 2 tr in last ch-2 sp, join with sl st to top of beg ch-3. (30 tr)
Round 4: Ch 3 (counts as 1 tr), [2 tr in next tr, 1 tr in next tr] 14 times, 2 tr in last tr, join with sl st to top of beg ch-3. (45 tr)
Round 5: *Skip next tr, 5 htr in next tr (petal made), skip next tr, sl st in next tr; rep from * around. (11 petals)
Fasten off and weave in ends.

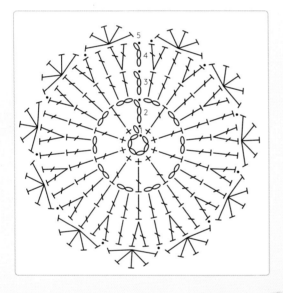

KEY
- ◯ Chain
- • Slip stitch
- + Double crochet
- ⊤ Half treble crochet
- ⊤ Treble crochet

CLINIC

WHAT DOES IT MEAN WHEN A PATTERN SAYS TO WORK INTO A CHAIN SPACE?

Making extra chains between stitches creates extra space for working the stitches of the following round. A space formed by two chains would be abbreviated to 'ch-2 sp' in a written pattern, as in this example. When a pattern instructs you to work into the chain space, the stitches should be made by inserting the hook into the space below the chain and not into the chains themselves. Chain spaces are used to create a variety of stitch patterns as well as to make the corners in crochet motifs such as granny squares (see page 64).

CROCHETING WITH STRING
This sample has been crocheted using string, which gives good stitch definition and texture, but it would look just as good in a cotton yarn.

This is a chain space ——————

MAKING A SPIRAL

Spirals can be made using any crochet stitch; this example uses double crochet. It is essential to mark the last stitch of each round or you will quickly lose your place. The best way to do this is to use a locking stitch marker, removing it each time you work the last stitch of a round and replacing it in the last stitch of each new round.

Stepped edge

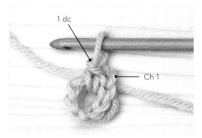

1 dc

Ch 1

STEP 1
Work the first round of stitches into the foundation ring (see page 56). Make one starting chain (this does not count as a stitch), then insert the hook into the centre of the ring and work the first double crochet stitch.

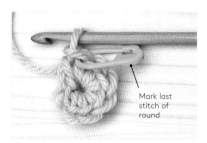

Mark last stitch of round

STEP 2
Make the required number of double crochets into the ring (6 dc in total in this example), but do not join the ends of the round with a slip stitch as you would when making a circle. Instead, mark the last stitch with a stitch marker.

CLINIC : HOW CAN I AVOID A STEPPED EDGE ON MY SPIRAL?

You can avoid the stepped edge on the final round of spirals by using a tapered finish. This is very useful when making spirals with taller stitches such as treble crochet, which often have a very pronounced stepped edge on the final round. Work to the marker indicating the last stitch of the final round, then make a series of shorter stitches to create a tapered edge. In the example below, a treble crochet spiral is finished with two half treble crochets in the last stitch of the round, one double crochet in the next stitch and a slip stitch in the following stitch. Fasten off in the usual way.

Move marker to last stitch of new round

STEP 3
Work the second round of stitches, increasing as specified in the pattern. Here, two double crochets are worked into each stitch on the previous round (12 dc in total). Remove the stitch marker when working the final two stitches of the round, then replace the marker in the last stitch of the round just finished.

STEP 4
For the next round, increase by working one double crochet in the next stitch and then two double crochets in the following stitch, repeating this sequence all around. At the end of the round, count the stitches; you should now have 18 dc. You can use the same principle of working increases evenly on each round to increase the size of the spiral.

Tapered finish

Blocks and motifs

Small shaped pieces of crochet, known as blocks or motifs, are popular with crocheters because they are small, portable and an ideal way to use up leftover yarn. In addition to circular motifs (see page 58), you can also create shapes such as squares, triangles and hexagons. Each of the shaped motifs in this section starts with a foundation ring (see page 56), which provides a secure start to the round and means your motifs are unlikely to unravel over time.

CHOOSING AND USING BLOCKS AND MOTIFS

Your starting point may be a favourite block you want to try, but you also need to consider what type of project it would be suitable for. For example, a solid block design would be best for a shopping bag rather than a lacier block, unless you are happy to add a fabric lining. Blocks can be fitted together in many different ways; the basic block arrangements are shown opposite. Make a few sample blocks to try out yarn and colour combinations and measure size, then draw a plan of the arrangement of blocks and count how many you will need to make. Use the sample blocks as a guide for calculating how much yarn to buy to make the whole project.

MAKING A PLAIN SQUARE BLOCK

Evenly spaced increases result in a flat, circular block, but when the increases are grouped together to make corners, the resulting block can be a square, hexagon, triangle or any other flat shape. Here, increases are grouped together at four corners to make a square block.

Join new yarn to any corner

Corner ch-2 sp

STEP 1
Follow the pattern (see opposite) to the end of round 1. You will now have four sets of ch-2 spaces. These form the four corner spaces of the block. Join the yarn for the next round into a corner space. The tie-in method of joining the yarn has been used here (see clinic, page 65), but you can use whichever method you prefer.

STEP 2
Follow the instructions for round 2, working 1 tr in each stitch along the sides of the square, but working an increase of 2 tr, ch 4, 2 tr in each corner space. Count the number of trebles along each side to make sure the sides are even.

STEP 3
On subsequent rounds, the increased tr stitches at the corners are worked into so that the sides of the square grow longer, but the central chain space at each corner remains the same. You can continue adding rounds in this way to make the square as big as you like.

CLINIC

IS THERE A DIFFERENCE BETWEEN A BLOCK AND A MOTIF?

Generally, any crochet that is not worked in a continuous piece is called a block. Blocks are usually a regular shape, such as a square or hexagon, and are designed to be repeated and joined together, rather like a fabric patchwork, to form a larger piece such as a blanket. Blocks can be worked back and forth in rows or in the round. The term motif is used interchangeably with the term block, but most commonly refers to small shapes – regular or irregular – worked in the round. Another term you might come across for a block or motif is medallion.

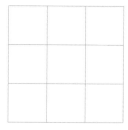

SQUARE
Join into horizontal or vertical strips, then join the strips together.

ROUND
Arrange in rows and sew together with a few stitches where the curves touch.

HEXAGONAL
Join into strips like square blocks. Work half blocks to fill the edges or leave them shaped if you prefer.

TRIANGULAR
Join into horizontal strips. When joining the strips together, pay particular attention to the points where the corners meet.

Plain square block
Worked in two colours, A and B.

Foundation ring: Using A, ch 6 and join with sl st to form a ring.
Round 1: Ch 5 (counts as 1 tr, ch 2), [3 tr into ring, ch 2] 3 times, 2 tr into ring, join with sl st to 3rd ch of beg ch-5. Fasten off A and join B in corner ch-2 sp.
Round 2: Ch 7 (counts as 1 tr, ch 4), 2 tr in same place, *1 tr in each of next 3 tr, (2 tr, ch 4, 2 tr) in next ch-2 sp; rep from * twice, 1 tr in each of next 2 tr, 1 tr in 3rd ch of beg ch-5 of previous round, 1 tr in next ch-2 sp, join with sl st to 3rd ch of beg ch-7.
Fasten off B and join A in corner ch-4 sp.

Round 3: Ch 7 (counts as 1 tr, ch 4), 2 tr in same place, *1 tr in each tr to next ch-4 sp, (2 tr, ch 4, 2 tr) in ch-4 sp; rep from * twice, 1 tr in each tr along fourth side, 1 tr in 3rd ch of beg ch-7 of previous round, 1 tr in next ch-4 sp, join with sl st to 3rd ch of beg ch-7.
Fasten off A and join B in corner ch-4 sp.
Round 4: As round 3.
Fasten off and weave in ends.

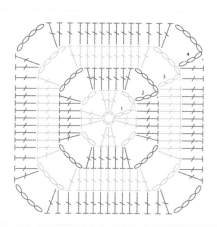

KEY
◯ Chain
• Slip stitch
T Treble crochet

GRANNY MOTIFS

The granny square is the most commonly recognised motif, and the design can also be worked in other shapes, such as triangles and hexagons (see page 66). Granny motifs are created by alternating groups of treble crochet stitches and chain stitches. All of the stitches on a granny motif are worked into chain spaces made on the previous round. Extra stitches and chains are worked at regular intervals to form the corners. Before you start each round, make sure you have worked the correct number of stitches and chains at each corner to keep the required shape.

MAKING A GRANNY SQUARE

First corner ch-3 sp

STEP 1
Start with a foundation ring of six chains joined with a slip stitch. To work the first round, make three chains for the starting chain, then work 2 tr, ch 3, 3 tr into the foundation ring. This creates the first corner.

STEP 2
Work [ch 3, 3 tr] twice, ch 3 into the ring, then join the round with a slip stitch in the usual way. You will now have four sets of ch-3 spaces. These form the four corner spaces of the block, and you will always work 3 tr, ch 3, 3 tr into these on each round.

STEP 3
Join the yarn colour for the second round into one of the corner chain spaces. The tie-in method of joining the yarn has been used here (see clinic, opposite), but you can use whichever method you prefer. Work the first corner of the second round as before.

Ch 1 along side between groups of 3 tr

STEP 4
Work ch 1 along the side of the motif, then work 3 tr, ch 3, 3 tr into the next corner ch-3 space. The ch 1 along the side forms a ch-1 space, and on all subsequent rounds you will increase the number of stitches along the sides by working 3 tr into each ch-1 space.

STEP 5
Continue to the end of the round and join together with a slip stitch. You will now have four corner ch-3 spaces and four ch-1 spaces along the sides.

STEP 6
Continue to work further rounds by following the principle of 3 tr, ch 3, 3 tr in each corner ch-3 space, and 3 tr in each ch-1 sp along the sides. Always work ch 1 before and after each set of 3 tr along the sides or the square will pucker and become misshapen. The number of ch-1 spaces will therefore increase on each round. So on the third round, for example, the number of ch-1 spaces on each side will increase to two.

CLINIC : HOW DO I CHANGE COLOURS WHEN MAKING MOTIFS?

There are several ways to change colours on each round of the motif. The simplest is to use a slip stitch join (see page 33), but you can try another technique known as the tie-in method.

STEP 1
Join the new yarn to any chain space by slipping the tail of the yarn through the chain space and tying it in a knot, leaving a 5cm (2in) tail (this can be woven in later).

STEP 2
Insert the hook from front to back into the chain space, pick up the working yarn, and make the number of starting chains specified in the pattern.

5 WAYS TO USE YOUR GRANNY SQUARES

1 Sew squares together to make a cushion cover.

2 Join squares into a long strip to make a colourful scarf.

3 Squares made of wool make ideal pot holders. The wool is insulating, so they are pretty and practical.

4 Make some motifs in colourful cotton and you will have a set of coasters for your coffee table.

5 Instead of making lots of little squares, try making one big square in colourful stripes.

Granny square
Worked in four colours, A, B, C and D.

Foundation ring: Using A, ch 6 and join with sl st to form a ring.

Round 1: Ch 3 (counts as 1 tr), 2 tr into ring, ch 3, [3 tr into ring, ch 3] 3 times, join with sl st to top of beg ch-3. Fasten off A and join B in corner ch-3 sp.

Round 2: Ch 3 (counts as 1 tr), (2 tr, ch 3, 3 tr) in same place, ch 1, *(3 tr, ch 3, 3 tr) in next ch-3 sp, ch 1; rep from * twice, join with sl st to top of beg ch-3. Fasten off B and join C in corner ch-3 sp.

Round 3: Ch 3 (counts as 1 tr), (2 tr, ch 3, 3 tr) in same place, ch 1, 3 tr in next ch-1 sp, ch 1, *(3 tr, ch 3, 3 tr) in next ch-3 sp, ch 1, 3 tr in next ch-1 sp, ch 1; rep from * twice, join with sl st to top of beg ch-3. Fasten off C and join D in corner ch-3 sp.

Round 4: Ch 3 (counts as 1 tr), (2 tr, ch 3, 3 tr) in same place, (ch 1, 3 tr) in each ch-1 sp along side of square, ch 1, *(3 tr, ch 3, 3 tr) in next corner ch-3 sp, (ch 1, 3 tr) in each ch-1 sp along side of square, ch 1; rep from * twice, join with sl st to top of beg ch-3. Fasten off and weave in ends.

KEY
○ Chain
• Slip stitch
⊤ Treble crochet

TRIANGLES AND HEXAGONS

The principles of the granny square (see page 64) can be applied to other shapes, such as triangles and hexagons. Simply by making three corners instead of four, you can create a pleasing triangle; make six corners and you will have a hexagon; make eight corners and you will have an octagon, and so on.

GRANNY TRIANGLE
Worked in three colours, A, B and C.

Foundation ring: Using A, ch 6 and join with sl st to form a ring.
Round 1: Ch 3 (counts as 1 tr), 2 tr into ring, ch 3, [3 tr into ring, ch 3] twice, join with sl st to top of beg ch-3.
Fasten off A and join B in corner ch-3 sp.
Round 2: Ch 3 (counts as 1 tr), (2 tr, ch 3, 3 tr) in same place, *ch 2, (3 tr, ch 3, 3 tr) in next ch-3 sp; rep from * once, ch 2, join with sl st to top of beg ch-3.
Fasten off B and join C in corner ch-3 sp.
Round 3: Ch 3 (counts as 1 tr), (2 tr, ch 3, 3 tr) in same place, ch 2, 3 tr in next ch-2 sp, *ch 2, (3 tr, ch 3, 3 tr) in next ch-3 sp, ch 2, 3 tr in next ch-2 sp; rep from * once, ch 2, join with sl st to top of beg ch-3.
Fasten off C and join B in corner ch-3 sp.
Round 4: Ch 3 (counts as 1 tr), (2 tr, ch 3, 3 tr) in same place, (ch 2, 3 tr) in each ch-2 sp along side of triangle, ch 2, *(3 tr, ch 3, 3 tr) in next corner ch-3 sp, (ch 2, 3 tr) in each ch-2 sp along side of triangle, ch 2; rep from * once, join with sl st to top of beg ch-3.
Fasten off and weave in ends.

GRANNY HEXAGON
Worked in three colours, A, B and C.

Foundation ring: Using A, ch 6 and join with sl st to form a ring.
Round 1: Ch 3 (counts as 1 tr), 2 tr into ring, ch 3, [3 tr into ring, ch 3] 5 times, join with sl st to top of beg ch-3.
Fasten off A and join B in corner ch-3 sp.
Round 2: Ch 3 (counts as 1 tr), (2 tr, ch 3, 3 tr) in same place, *ch 1, (3 tr, ch 3, 3 tr) in next ch-3 sp; rep from * 4 times, ch 1, join with sl st to top of beg ch-3.
Fasten off B and join C in corner ch-3 sp.
Round 3: Ch 3 (counts as 1 tr), (2 tr, ch 3, 3 tr) in same place, *ch 1, 3 tr in next ch-1 sp, ch 1, (3 tr, ch 3, 3 tr) in next ch-3 sp; rep from * 4 times, ch 1, 3 tr in next ch-1 sp, ch 1, join with sl st to top of beg ch-3.
Fasten off and weave in ends.

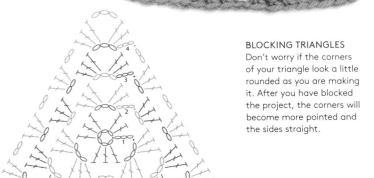

BLOCKING TRIANGLES
Don't worry if the corners of your triangle look a little rounded as you are making it. After you have blocked the project, the corners will become more pointed and the sides straight.

KEY
◯ Chain
• Slip stitch
T Treble
  crochet

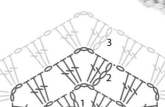

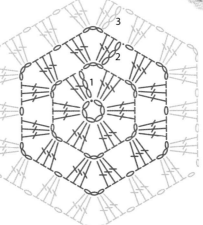

MAKING A CIRCLE IN A SQUARE

You can create stunning motifs by combining different shapes, and rounded shapes within a square frame are particularly effective. The circle within a square is a lovely motif for blankets and homewares.

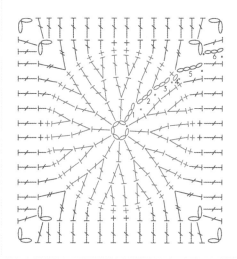

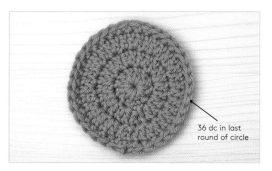

36 dc in last round of circle

STEP 1
Follow the pattern to the end of round 4 to complete the circle (see right). Count the stitches to make sure you have 36 double crochet.

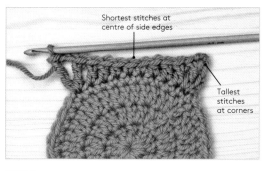

Shortest stitches at centre of side edges

Tallest stitches at corners

STEP 2
Join yarn B to any double crochet and make 6 chains as directed (this counts as the first double treble plus 2 chains at the first corner). Make a double treble in the same place as the 6 chains to complete the first corner, then follow the sequence of stitches as written in the pattern. You will see the square beginning to form by the use of taller stitches at the corners and progressively shorter stitches towards the centre of the side edge.

STEP 3
When you complete round 5, you will see that the circle is now framed within a square. Count the stitches to make sure each side has the same number because it is easy to miss a stitch. On the last round, a treble is made into each stitch to create a solid frame.

Circle in a square
Worked in two colours, A and B.

Foundation ring: Using A, ch 6 and join with sl st to form a ring.
Round 1: Ch 3 (counts as 1 tr), 11 tr into ring, join with sl st to top of beg ch-3. (12 tr)
Round 2: Ch 3 (counts as 1 tr), 1 tr in same place, 2 tr in each of next 11 tr, join with sl st to top of beg ch-3. (24 tr)
Round 3: Ch 3 (counts as 1 tr), 1 tr in same place, 1 tr in next tr, [2 tr in next tr, 1 tr in next tr] 11 times, join with sl st to top of beg ch-3. (36 tr)
Round 4: Ch 1, 1 dc in each tr around, join with sl st to first dc. (36 dc)
Fasten off A and join B to any dc.
Round 5: Ch 6 (counts as 1 dtr, ch 2), 1 dtr in same place, *1 tr in each of next 2 dc, 1 htr in next dc, 1 dc in each of next 2 dc, 1 htr in next dc, 1 tr in each of next 2 dc**, (1 dtr, ch 2, 1 dtr) in next dc; rep from * twice, then from * to ** once, join with sl st to 4th ch of beg ch-6. (40 sts, 4 ch sp corners)
Round 6: Sl st into corner ch-2 sp, ch 3 (counts as 1 tr), (1 tr, ch 2, 2 tr) in same place, *1 tr in each st to next corner ch-2 sp, (2 tr, ch 2, 2 tr) in ch-2 sp; rep from * twice, 1 tr in each st to last corner ch-2 sp, join with sl st to top of beg ch-3.
Fasten off and weave in ends.

MAKING A FLOWER IN A SQUARE

This flower framed in a square is a very pretty motif designed to practise several techniques. Although more complex than the previous motifs, it is simpler than it first appears.

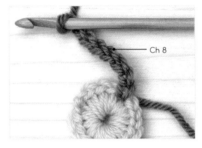

STEP 1
Follow the pattern to the end of round 1 (see opposite). This forms the centre of the flower. Join yarn B (petal colour) to any stitch on the first round, then make 8 chains.

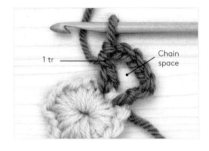

STEP 2
Skip the next stitch of round 1 and work a treble crochet into the next stitch. This makes the first chain space for adding the petals on the next round. Continue in this way until you have 8 tr and 8 ch sp.

STEP 3
Make a slip stitch into the next chain space, ready to add the first petal. Following round 3 of the pattern, work all the stitches inside the square brackets into the same chain space. The stitches range in height, becoming progressively taller towards the centre to create the petal shape. Make the stitches for the next petal into the next chain space.

STEP 4
Make eight petals in total, one in each chain space. Each petal has a central chain space. This is where you will join the yarn for working the square frame.

STEP 5
Join yarn C into one of the chain spaces at the centre of a petal. Follow round 4 of the pattern. At the end of the round, you will have made a circle, with loops of chain stitches joined to the tip of each petal.

STEP 6
Work round 5 of the pattern. This is the round that makes the circular chain into a square frame. Double crochet stitches are worked into each chain space all around the motif, but with a few extra stitches and a ch-3 space at each of the four corners to create a square shape.

STEP 7
Here, you can see the final round in progress. Each treble is worked into a double crochet on the previous round to create a square frame with solid edges, and the corners are made with a series of trebles and chains. The finished result is a very pretty motif.

Flower in a square

Worked in three colours, A, B and C.

Foundation ring: Using A, ch 8 and join with sl st to form a ring.

Round 1: Ch 1, 16 dc into ring, join with sl st to first dc. Fasten off A and join B to any dc.

Round 2: Ch 8 (counts as 1 tr, ch 5), [skip next dc, 1 tr in next dc, ch 5] 7 times, join with sl st to 3rd ch of beg ch-8.

Round 3: Sl st into next ch-5 sp, [(1 dc, 1 htr, 2 tr, 1 dtr, ch 1, 1 dtr, 2 tr, 1 htr, 1 dc) in ch-5 sp] 8 times, join with sl st to first dc. Fasten off B and join C to any ch-1 sp.

Round 4: Ch 1, 1 dc in same place, *ch 7, 1 dc in next ch-1 sp, ch 9**, 1 dc in next ch-1 sp; rep from * twice, then from * to ** once, join with sl st to first dc.

Round 5: Sl st into first ch-7 sp, ch 1, *7 dc in ch-7 sp, (6 dc, ch 3, 6 dc) in next ch-9 sp; rep from * 3 times, join with sl st to first dc.

Round 6: Ch 3 (counts as 1 tr), *1 tr in each dc to next ch-3 sp, (2 tr, ch 3, 2 tr) in ch-3 sp; rep from * 3 times, 1 tr in each of next 6 dc, join with sl st to top of beg ch-3.

Fasten off and weave in ends.

COTTON VARIATION

The main block (above right) is worked in a wool yarn, while the block below is worked in a cotton yarn, which gives clearer stitch definition. This block has also been worked using a subtle variation in technique by omitting the starting chain when a round begins with a double crochet stitch (rounds 1, 4 and 5). Some designers see it as superfluous when working in rounds because straight edges are not needed, especially if it follows a slip stitch.

KEY

- ⌒ Chain
- • Slip stitch
- + Double crochet
- ⊤ Half treble crochet
- ┃ Treble crochet
- ‡ Double treble crochet

4 WAYS TO USE CROCHET MOTIFS

1. Sew several motifs together to make a scarf or wrap.

2. Make a blanket by sewing lots of motifs together (see page 43) or joining with a double crochet seam (see page 45). Motifs with firm edges are ideal for this.

3. Using the quick start granny square cushion as a guide (see page 72), make a granny square blanket by joining several squares to make strips, then join the strips together. Or why not make the cushion but use a different square motif instead?

4. Sew your motifs on to a length of ribbon or a strip of double crochet to make colourful bunting. The granny triangle (page 66) would be perfect for this.

Tubular crochet

Tubular crochet is worked in the round, starting with a length of chain joined into a ring. The tube or cylinder can be as wide or as narrow as you wish. The first round of stitches is worked into the chains rather than into the ring, just as when working in rows.

DOUBLE CROCHET SPIRAL CYLINDER

The easiest of all the crochet cylinders is a double crochet tube worked without starting chains. This technique is the foundation of most amigurumi patterns, often used to produce the limbs as three-dimensional rather than as flat pieces, which eliminates the need for seams.

STEP 1
Ch 20 and join with a slip stitch to form a ring, making sure the chains are not twisted.

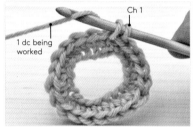

STEP 2
Ch 1 (this does not count as a stitch), then work the first double crochet in the same place as the slip stitch. Work one double crochet in each chain until you reach the last chain.

STEP 3
After making a double crochet in the last chain, place a stitch marker in this stitch to keep track of each round. Begin the next round by working one double crochet in each stitch. Continue to work around until the tube is the desired length, moving the marker into the last stitch of each round as you progress.

STEP 4
As the spiral grows, you will see that the beginning of the round moves gradually to the right.

TREBLE CROCHET CYLINDER

Use these techniques when working taller stitches than double crochet; these examples use treble crochet. There will be a seam running up the cylinder. If you turn the work after each round, the seam will be straight. If you don't, the seam will spiral around the cylinder.

WITHOUT TURNS

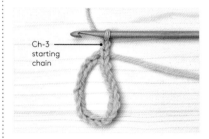

STEP 1
Ch 20 and join with a slip stitch to form a ring, making sure the chains are not twisted. Make three chains for the starting chain; this counts as the first treble crochet stitch.

STEP 2
Make one treble into each chain until you reach the end of the round.

REASONS TO TRY TUBULAR CROCHET TODAY

3

1 Practise the technique and you will soon be ready to try your first amigurumi toy pattern (see page 76).

2 These cute crochet characters are made using basic crochet skills but look more complex, so you can impress your friends with your newfound crochet skills.

3 You only need small scraps of yarn, so there is little financial outlay.

WITH TURNS

STEP 3
Join the round with a slip stitch into the top of the starting chain. To start the next round, make three starting chains (counts as 1 tr), skip the first treble and then work 1 tr in each stitch around. Join the round with a slip stitch into the top of the starting chain.

STEP 1
Work steps 1–2 of making a treble crochet cylinder without turns until the last stitch of the first round. Join the round with a slip stitch.

STEP 2
Turn the cylinder to reverse the direction of your work. Make three chains; these count as the first stitch. Skip the first treble and then make one treble in each stitch to the end of the round.

STEP 4
Continue working in rounds until the cylinder is the desired length. You can see the seam spiralling around the cylinder.

STEP 3
Join the round by making a slip stitch into the top of the starting chain. Turn the work again and work another round. Remember to make a starting chain and skip the first stitch of each round.

STEP 4
Continue to work as many rounds as stated in the pattern. You can see the seam running straight up the cylinder.

Quick
start
project:

Granny square cushion

One side of this pretty cushion is made from
16 small granny squares joined together,
while the other side is worked as one big
granny square, but you could make both
sides the same if you prefer. Indulge your
love of colour or go for a more neutral scheme
like this one.

FINISHED SIZE
To fit a 40cm (16in) square cushion pad
Each small granny square measures 9.5cm (3³/₄in) square

TENSION
Make the first small square and check against stated dimensions;
if necessary, adjust size of hook if you want to match stated size.

YOU WILL NEED
- 1 x 50g ball of DK-weight wool yarn in each of yellow (A),
  pink (B), mauve (C) and beige (D); Tracey used DMC Woolly,
  100% merino wool with approx. 125m (136yd) per ball, in
  092 (A), 042 (B), 062 (C) and 111 (D), but any DK yarn can
  be substituted
- 4mm crochet hook
- Yarn needle
- 40cm (16in) square cushion pad

ABBREVIATIONS AND TECHNIQUES
ch = chain (page 18)
dc = double crochet (page 23)
sl st = slip stitch (page 22)
sp = space
tr = treble crochet (page 25)
WS = wrong side
Starting the round (page 56)
Making a granny square (page 64)
Double crochet seam (page 45)

PATTERN NOTES
- Both sides of the cushion are made using the same granny
  square motif pattern on page 65. Simply repeat round 4 of
  the pattern to make the granny square as large as you wish.
- The small motifs are joined together using a double crochet
  seam, and then the two sides of the cushion are joined together
  using the same method. If you prefer, you can sew all the seams
  instead (see page 43).

SIDE A
Using the granny square motif pattern, make
16 granny squares in the following colour sequence:
Round 1: Yarn A.
Round 2: Yarn B.
Round 3: Yarn C.
Round 4: Yarn D.
Weave in ends as you complete each motif.
Using a double crochet seam, join the squares together
into strips of four, then join the strips together to make
a square.
Edging: Join yarn D to any corner ch-3 sp, then work
3 dc in each corner ch-3 sp, 1 dc in each tr and 1 dc in
each ch-1 sp around perimeter of cushion, join with sl st
to first dc.

SIDE B
Use the same granny square motif pattern to make one
large square by working rounds 1–4 as instructed, and
then repeat round 4 to work 16 rounds in total using
the following colour sequence:
Round 1: Yarn A.
Round 2: Yarn B.
Round 3: Yarn C.
Rounds 4–15: Repeat colour sequence of one round
each in yarns A, B and C four times more.
Round 16: Yarn D.
Fasten off and weave in ends.

TO FINISH
With WS together, pin front and back together on three
sides. Join yarn D to any dc. Inserting hook through
corresponding dc of both front and back pieces, work
1 dc in each dc around all three sides. Remove pins,
insert cushion pad and join remaining side in the same
way. Fasten off and weave in ends.

Quick
start
project:

Beanie hat

This simple beanie can be worn by any person of any age. It can easily be adapted to your own size and colour preferences. You can make the pompom any size you like, or omit it if you prefer.

FINISHED SIZE

Small: 23cm (9in) long; to fit head circumference up to 50cm (19³/₄in)

Medium/large: 27cm (10³/₄in) long; to fit head circumference up to 55cm (21³/₄in)

Length is adjustable

TENSION

16 sts and 8 rows = 10cm (4in) square over treble crochet; first five rounds measure 10cm (4in) in diameter

YOU WILL NEED

• 1 x 50g ball of DK-weight wool yarn in each of beige (A) and yellow (B); Tracey used DMC Woolly, 100% merino wool with approx. 125m (136yd) per ball, in 111 (A) and 093 (B), but any DK yarn with a high wool content can be substituted
• 4mm crochet hook
• Yarn needle
• Pompom maker (or use two cardboard circles)

ABBREVIATIONS AND TECHNIQUES

ch = chain (page 18)
dc = double crochet (page 23)
rep = repeat
sl st = slip stitch (page 22)
st(s) = stitch(es)
tr = treble crochet (page 25)
Starting the round (page 56)
Increasing (page 37)
Joining yarn (page 32)

PATTERN NOTES

• Ch 3 at the beginning of a round counts as the first treble crochet stitch. Ch 1 at the beginning of a round does not count as a stitch.
• The pattern begins at the top of the hat. When you reach the stripe sequence, do not fasten off yarns when changing colours; carry the unused yarn between stripes.
• Instructions for both sizes are the same until round 7. After this, instructions for the small size are given first, with the larger size in parentheses – small(medium/large).
• To make the hat longer, simply work more rounds in treble crochet before beginning the double crochet stripe sequence. To make the hat shorter, worker fewer treble crochet rounds.

HAT

Foundation ring: Using A, ch 4 and join with sl st to form a ring.

Round 1: Ch 3, 9 tr into ring, join with sl st to top of beg ch-3. (10 sts)

Round 2: Ch 3, 1 tr in same place, 2 tr in each st around, join with sl st to top of beg ch-3. (20 sts)

Round 3: Ch 3, 2 tr in next st, *1 tr in each of next 2 sts, 2 tr in next st; rep from * to end, join with sl st to top of beg ch-3. (30 sts)

Round 4: Ch 3, 1 tr in next st, 2 tr in next st, *1 tr in each of next 2 sts, 2 tr in next st; rep from * to end, join with sl st to top of beg ch-3. (40 sts)

Round 5: Ch 3, 1 tr in each of next 2 sts, 2 tr in next st, *1 tr in each of next 3 sts, 2 tr in next st; rep from * to end, join with sl st to top of beg ch-3. (50 sts)

Round 6: Ch 3, 1 tr in each of next 3 sts, 2 tr in next st, *1 tr in each of next 4 sts, 2 tr in next st; rep from * to end, join with sl st to top of beg ch-3. (60 sts)

Round 7: Ch 3, 1 tr in each of next 4 sts, 2 tr in next st, *1 tr in each of next 5 sts, 2 tr in next st; rep from * to end, join with sl st to top of beg ch-3. (70 sts)

Medium/large only:

Round 8: Ch 3, 1 tr in each of next 4 sts, 2 tr in next st, *1 tr in each of next 5 sts, 2 tr in next st; rep from * to end, join with sl st to top of beg ch-3. (80 sts)

Both sizes:

Rounds 8–17(9–19): Ch 3, 1 tr in each st around, join with sl st to top of beg ch-3.

Round 18(20): Ch 1, 1 dc in each st around, join with sl st to beg ch-1. (70[80]sts)

Round 19(21): Ch 1, 1 dc in each st around, join with sl st to beg ch-1.

Rounds 20–21(22–23): Using B, ch 1, 1 dc in each st around, join with sl st to beg ch-1.

Rounds 22–29(24–31): Continue working in double crochet as for round 19(21), alternating two rounds in each colour.

Fasten off and weave in ends.

Using B, make a pompom and sew securely to top of hat.

Guest Designer Stephanie Lau

My name is Stephanie Lau, and I've been crocheting ever since I was a little girl. I rediscovered my love of crochet when I got married and started working, and I absolutely fell in love with amigurumi, the Japanese art of knitted/crocheted stuffed animals. This love of amigurumi drove me to start my blog 'All About Ami' in January 2011, and I've been documenting my projects and sharing my original designs with people all over the world ever since. I live in Alberta, Canada, with my loving husband Ryan, who helps me photograph, design and complete my projects, and I am also the mommy to two sweet little girls named Myla and Brielle. You can follow my work at www.AllAboutAmi.com.

Finnley the fox

Finnley is a sweet fox who is sure to bring a smile to everyone's face with his adorable expression, rosy cheeks and big bushy tail. He loves playing hide and seek, snuggling up with a good book and also creating a little bit of mischief. Crochet this little foxy friend for yourself and you will be in for a treat.

FINISHED SIZE
Height: 15cm (6in) to top of ears
Width: 10cm (4in) at base

TENSION
Accurate tension is not essential for this project; the first 5 rounds of the head in double crochet measure 1³/₈ in. (3.5 cm) in diameter on sample shown

YOU WILL NEED
• 1 x 50g ball of 4ply-weight cotton yarn in each of red (A), white (B) and black (C); Stephanie chose DMC Natura Just Cotton, 100% cotton with approx. 155m (170yd) per ball, in Coral N18, Ibiza N01 and Noir N11
• 2mm crochet hook
• Pair of 6mm safety eyes
• 2 pink brads for cheeks
• Toy stuffing
• Black embroidery thread
• Yarn needle
• Sheet of white felt
• Glue gun

ABBREVIATIONS AND TECHNIQUES
ch = chain (page 18)
dc = double crochet (page 23)
dc2tog = double crochet 2 together (see pattern notes)
sl st = slip stitch (page 22)
st(s) = stitch(es)
tbl = through back loop (page 84)
Magic ring (pages 56–57)
Joining yarn (page 32)
Shaping (page 36–39)
Tubular crochet (page 70)

PATTERN NOTES
• The nose tab is worked in rows, but all other parts of the fox are worked in rounds of tubular crochet to form a double crochet spiral cylinder. Take care to work in continuous rounds to form a spiral, otherwise a seam will show. Use a stitch marker to help you keep track of each round.
• Wherever the pattern requires a decrease (dc2tog), use the invisible decrease method for a cleaner look and less visible holes (see clinic, opposite).

• When attaching limbs and ears, make sure that the colour changes are positioned towards the back of the toy for a neater look (see page 78).
• Templates are provided for cutting the felt pieces for the ears and belly (see page 78), but these are only a guide. Everyone's fox will probably turn out a slightly different size, which is very common with amigurumi, so adjust the size to suit your fox.
• Refer to the nose stitch guide for how to embroider the triangular nose using embroidery thread (see page 78).

NOSE TAB

Foundation chain: Using A and leaving a long end for sewing nose tab to head, ch 3.

Row 1: 1 dc in second ch from hook, 1 dc in next ch, turn. (2 sts)

Row 2: Ch 1, [3 dc in next st] twice, turn. (6 sts)

Row 3: Ch 1, 1 dc in each st to end, turn.

Row 4: Ch 1, 2 dc in first st, 1 dc in each of next 4 sts, 2 dc in last st. (8 sts)

Fasten off.

HEAD

Using B, make a magic ring.

Round 1: 6 dc into ring. (6 sts)

Round 2: 2 dc in each st around. (12 sts)

Round 3: [1 dc in next st, 2 dc in next st] 6 times. (18 sts)

Round 4: [1 dc in each of next 2 sts, 2 dc in next st] 6 times. (24 sts)

Round 5: [1 dc in each of next 3 sts, 2 dc in next st] 6 times. (30 sts)

Round 6: [1 dc in each of next 4 sts, 2 dc in next st] 6 times. (36 sts)

Round 7: [1 dc in each of next 5 sts, 2 dc in next st] 6 times. (42 sts)

Round 8: [1 dc in each of next 6 sts, 2 dc in next st] 6 times. (48 sts)

Round 9: [1 dc in each of next 7 sts, 2 dc in next st] 6 times. (54 sts)

Round 10: [1 dc in each of next 8 sts, 2 dc in next st] 6 times. (60 sts)

Rounds 11–12: 1 dc in each st around.

Round 13: 1 dc in each of next 23 sts, [2 dc in next st, 1 dc in each of next 3 sts] 3 times, 2 dc in next st, 1 dc in each of next 24 sts. (64 sts)

Rounds 14–17: 1 dc in each st around. Change to A and create a hole where the nose tab will be attached to form the snout as follows.

Round 18: 1 dc in each of next 28 sts, ch 6, skip 11 sts, 1 dc in each of next 25 sts. (53 dc and 6 ch)

Round 19: 1 dc in each of next 28 sts, 1 dc tbl in each of next 6 ch, 1 dc in each of next 25 sts. (59 sts)

Rounds 20–27: 1 dc in each st around.

Round 28: [1 dc in each of next 8 sts, dc2tog] 5 times, 1 dc in each of next 9 sts. (54 sts)

Round 29: [1 dc in each of next 7 sts, dc2tog] 6 times. (48 sts)

Round 30: [1 dc in each of next 6 sts, dc2tog] 6 times. (42 sts)

Round 31: [1 dc in each of next 5 sts, dc2tog] 6 times. (36 sts)

Place safety eyes at the junction of yarns A and B between rounds 17 and 18, about 3 stitches outwards from the nose hole on either side.

For cheeks, place pink brads between rounds 15 and 16 diagonally downwards and outwards from eyes.

Begin stuffing head.

Sew nose tab to head to form snout. Embroider the nose using black embroidery thread in a triangle shape.

Round 32: [1 dc in each of next 4 sts, dc2tog] 6 times. (30 sts)

Round 33: [1 dc in each of next 3 sts, dc2tog] 6 times. (24 sts)

Round 34: [1 dc in each of next 2 sts, dc2tog] 6 times. (18 sts)

Round 35: 1 dc in next st, dc2tog] 6 times. (12 sts)

Finish stuffing head.

Round 36: [Dc2tog] 6 times. (6 sts)

Fasten off and weave in ends.

EARS (MAKE 2)

Using C, make a magic ring.

Round 1: 4 dc into ring. (4 sts)

Round 2: 1 dc in each st around.

Round 3: 2 dc in each st around. (8 sts)

Round 4: [1 dc in next st, 2 dc in next st] 4 times. (12 sts)

Change to A.

Round 5: [1 dc in each of next 5 sts, 2 dc in next st] twice. (14 sts)

Round 6: [1 dc in each of next 6 sts, 2 dc in next st] twice. (16 sts)

Round 7: [1 dc in each of next 7 sts, 2 dc in next st] twice. (18 sts)

Rounds 8–10: 1 dc in each st around.

Round 11: [1 dc in each of next 7 sts, dc2tog] twice. (16 sts)

Round 12: 1 dc in each st around.

Each ear has slightly different instructions for next round so that they can be attached more cleanly to the curves of the head.

Round 13 (right ear only): Ch 1, turn, starting in second st from hook, 1 dc in each of next 8 sts.

Round 13 (left ear only): Sl st in next st, (sl st, ch 1, 1 dc) in next st, 1 dc in each of next 7 sts.

Fasten off, leaving long end for sewing. Fold ears so that colour changes are positioned towards the back and the stitches worked on round 13 are folded in half. These stitches should be positioned on the outer edge of the ears to help attach the ears more cleanly to the curve of the head. Cut out ear lining from white felt and glue lining on to ears. Sew ears to top of head.

CLINIC

HOW DO YOU WORK AN INVISIBLE DECREASE?

STEP 1
Work to the instruction dc2tog, then insert the hook into the front loop only of the next stitch (2 loops on hook).

STEP 2
Insert the hook into the front loop only of the following stitch (3 loops on hook).

STEP 3
Wrap the yarn over the hook and draw it through the first two loops on the hook. Wrap the yarn over the hook again and draw it through the remaining two loops on the hook to complete the decrease.

BODY

Using A, make a magic ring and work first 6 rounds as for head.
Round 7: 1 dc tbl in each st around.
Rounds 8–12: 1 dc in each st around.
Round 13: [1 dc in each of next 4 sts, dc2tog] 6 times. (30 sts)
Rounds 14–18: 1 dc in each st around.
Round 19: [1 dc in each of next 3 sts, dc2tog] 6 times. (24 sts)
Round 20: 1 dc in each st around.
Fasten off, leaving long end for sewing.
Stuff body and sew to head.
Cut out belly lining from white felt and glue to body.

ARMS (MAKE 2)

Using C, make a magic ring.
Round 1: 6 dc into ring. (6 sts)
Round 2: 2 dc in each st around. (12 sts)
Round 3: 1 dc in each st around.
Round 4: 1 dc tbl in each st around.
Rounds 5–6: As round 3.
Change to A.
Rounds 7–8: As round 3.
Round 9: [1 dc in each of next 4 sts, dc2tog] twice. (10 sts)
Rounds 10–16: As round 3.
Fasten off, leaving long end for sewing.
Stuff lightly. Pinch open end together and sew shut. Attach to sides of body.
Optional: After sewing all the parts together (arms, legs and tail on to body), sew paws together in front of body for better posing and sitting.

LEGS (MAKE 2)

Using C, make a magic ring and work first 6 rounds as for arms.
Change to A.
Rounds 7–13: As round 3.
Round 14: [1 dc in each of next 4 sts, dc2tog] twice. (10 sts)
Rounds 15–17: As round 3.
Fasten off, leaving long end for sewing.
Stuff lightly. Pinch open end together and sew shut. Attach to sides of body.

TAIL

Using B, make a magic ring.
Round 1: 4 dc into ring. (4 sts)
Round 2: 1 dc in each st around.
Round 3: [1 dc in next st, 2 dc in next st] twice. (6 sts)
Round 4: 2 dc in each st around. (12 sts)
Round 5: As round 2.
Round 6: 2 dc in each of the next 6 sts, 1 dc in each of the next 6 sts. (18 sts)
Round 7: As round 2.
Round 8: 1 dc in each of next 3 sts, 2 dc in each of next 6 sts, 1 dc in each of next 9 sts. (24 sts)
Rounds 9–11: As round 2.
Round 12: 2 dc in each of next 2 sts, 1 dc in each of next 18 sts, 2 dc in each of next 4 sts. (30 sts)
Round 13: As round 2.
Round 14: 2 dc in each of next 2 sts, 1 dc in each of next 24 sts, 2 dc in each of next 4 sts. (36 sts)
Rounds 15–17: As round 2.

Change to A.
Round 18: 2 dc in next st, 1 dc in each of next 30 sts, 2 dc in each of next 5 sts. (42 sts)
Round 19: As round 2.
Round 20: 1 dc in each of next 36 sts, 2 dc in each of next 6 sts. (48 sts)
Rounds 21–30: As round 2.
Round 31: [1 dc in each of next 6 sts, dc2tog] 6 times. (42 sts)
Round 32: [1 dc in each of next 5 sts, dc2tog] 6 times. (36 sts)
Round 33: [1 dc in each of next 4 sts, dc2tog] 6 times. (30 sts)
Round 34: [1 dc in each of next 3 sts, dc2tog] 6 times. (24 sts)
Begin stuffing tail.
Round 35: [1 dc in each of next 2 sts, dc2tog] 6 times. (18 sts)
Round 36: [1 dc in next st, dc2tog] 6 times. (12 sts)
Finish stuffing tail.
Round 37: [Dc2tog] 6 times. (6 sts)
Fasten off, leaving long end for sewing.
Bring long end of A to right side between rounds 28 and 29 (nine rounds up from bottom of tail) and attach tail to back of fox.

FRONT OF EARS

Long ends for sewing to head

Round 13 stitches folded towards outside

BACK OF EARS

Colour changes face towards back

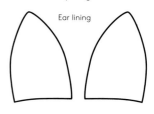

Belly lining

Ear lining

Nose stitch
Bring the tapestry needle to the front of the work at 1, take it through to the back at 2 to form a horizontal stitch and then bring it through to the front again at 3 to start embroidering a triangle of vertical stitches.

Be inspired

1. 'HAVE FUN' CROCHET NECKLACE, RASA GRIGAITE
Starting from a foundation ring, a series of increases and decreases has been used to create a round bead. Threading a selection of harmonious colours on to a simple wire creates a stunning piece of jewellery.

2. BLANKET, SANDRA PAUL
Bold colours have been used to crochet the motifs for this blanket. The motifs are joined together using a double crochet seam, and a decorative edging completes the blanket. By using the same colour for the last round of each motif and for the edging, the designer has transformed a simple motif blanket into an heirloom piece.

3. PONCHO, SANDRA PAUL
This poncho is worked in one piece using the tubular crochet method.

A variety of stitches have been used to shape the piece, and the palette of harmonious colours has upgraded the traditional crochet poncho into a modern, wearable accessory.

4. DRAGON, STEPHANIE LAU
The designer has used simple amigurumi techniques (magic circle and invisible decreases) to make a quirky dragon. Using felt, plastic eyes and embroidery embellishments gives the amigurumi a unique character and personality.

5. CHRISTMAS BAUBLES,
KATE GREEN
Starting with a foundation ring, simple increases have been used to create the two halves of the rounded bauble shape, sewn together over a glass bauble. The combination of bright and traditional colours makes an attractive and modern decoration.

6. CAPELET, SANDRA PAUL
The tiny motifs that make up this pretty capelet have been joined on the last round of each motif, and then a crochet strip has been added in stripes to enhance the motifs. A drawstring at the neck allows the shape to be altered to fit the wearer.

7. FLOWER HEADBAND,
SIDSEL J. HØIVIK
This pretty headband shows how small flowers and motifs can be used to great effect. A crochet chain has been used to make the garland, with a variety of motifs attached.

8. POUFFE AND RUG,
DAVID SOARES OLIVEIRA
The doily-style rug makes a stunning addition to a modern decor and is achieved using jumbo yarns and a large hook. The pouffe is worked in rounds, with textured stitches used to add interest. Modern crochet designers use vibrant colours to bring traditional techniques such as the doily to a new audience.

CHAPTER 3

Stitch Patterns

Once you are comfortable with the basic crochet stitches and techniques, you can start to experiment and extend your skills. There are countless ways to add interest to your crochet and this chapter explores different ways to add texture, colour and visual detail. If you are already confident with making the basic stitches, this chapter is the ideal place to dip in and try some new techniques.

Simple stitch variations

A few simple variations on the standard stitches can give your crochet a completely different look. For example, by inserting the hook into a different part of the stitch, or by adding extra yarnovers, you can create interesting and useful effects without too much difficulty.

WORKING INTO ONE LOOP

Most crochet stitches are worked by inserting the hook under both of the loops that lie along the top of the stitch you are working into. By inserting the hook into only one of these loops, you can create an attractive texture. You can use this technique with any of the basic stitches; these examples use double crochet. A standard double crochet is sometimes worked into the first and last stitches of each row to give the crochet extra stability and make a stronger edge for sewing seams or adding an edging.

BACK LOOP

STEP 1

Work into each stitch of the row in the usual way, but insert the hook under the back loop only instead of under both loops at the top of the stitch. The back loop is the one farthest from you as you work the row (not necessarily the loop nearest the wrong side of the work).

STEP 2

Continue across the row, working into the back loops only. After two or three rows, you will see the characteristic ridges formed by the unworked front loops. In double crochet this is sometimes called horizontal ribbing. Remember that you can insert the hook under both loops of the first and last stitches of the row if a more stable edge is required.

FRONT LOOP

STEP 1

Work into each stitch of the row in the usual way, but insert the hook under the front loop only instead of under both loops at the top of the stitch. Working into the front loops makes an open, lacy fabric with lots of drape. The front loop is the one nearest you as you work the row (not necessarily the loop nearest the right side of the work).

STEP 2

Continue across the row, working into the front loops only. After a few rows, you will be able to see the texture of the fabric and notice how it differs from both standard and back loop double crochet. As with back loop crochet, working under both loops for the first and last stitches will create a stronger edge.

EXTENDED STITCHES

Extended stitches are taller, slightly elongated and looser versions of the standard crochet stitches. They are all made by working an extra yarnover. They make loose, flexible stitches, and fabric that has plenty of drape. They are sometimes referred to as locked stitches or Elmore stitches. They are often used to transition from a shorter stitch to a taller stitch, such as when shaping corners. This example shows extended double crochet, but the same technique can be used with all the basic stitches.

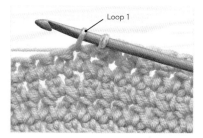

STEP 1
Work the first stage of the stitch in the usual way. For double crochet, insert the hook into the next stitch, wrap the yarn over the hook and draw a loop through to the front.

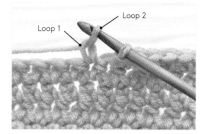

STEP 2
Wrap the yarn over the hook again and pull it through one loop on the hook. This is the extra yarnover that creates the extended stitch and leaves you with the same number of loops on the hook.

STEP 3
Complete the stitch in the usual way. For double crochet, wrap the yarn over the hook again and pull it through both loops on the hook.

Alternate loops

Foundation chain: Make any number of ch + 1.
Row 1: 1 dc in second ch from hook, 1 dc in each ch to end, turn.
Row 2: Ch 1, 1 dc in front loop of each dc to end, turn.
Row 3: Ch 1, 1 dc in back loop of each dc to end, turn.
Repeat rows 2–3 for pattern.

KEY
⟳ Chain
⊥ Double crochet in front loop
⟂ Double crochet in back loop

Extended double crochet

Foundation chain: Make any number of ch + 2.
Row 1: 1 Exdc in third ch from hook, 1 Exdc in each ch to end, turn.
Row 2: Ch 2 (counts as 1 Exdc), skip first Exdc, 1 Exdc in each Exdc to end, working last Exdc in top of beg ch-2, turn.
Repeat row 2 for pattern.

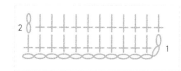

KEY
⟳ Chain
┼ Extended double crochet

Raised and relief stitches

Raised or post stitches are made by inserting the hook around the post of the stitch below instead of under the top loops. Raised stitches are usually worked into the taller stitches, such as treble crochet, which have a longer post (sometimes called a stem). Crossed stitches can pass in front or behind each other, creating an effect similar to knitted cables, while spike stitches are worked over other stitches into a different row.

FRONT POST STITCHES

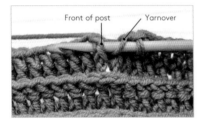

STEP 1
This example uses treble crochet, so start by wrapping the yarn over the hook once. Working from the front of the crochet fabric, insert the hook and take it around the post of the stitch on the row below from right to left. Bring the hook through to the front of the fabric again.

STEP 2
Wrap the yarn over the hook, draw a loop through and complete the treble crochet stitch in the usual way.

BACK POST STITCHES

STEP 1
This example uses treble crochet, so start by wrapping the yarn over the hook once. Working from the back of the crochet fabric, insert the hook and take it around the post of the stitch on the row below from right to left. Take the hook through to the back of the fabric again.

STEP 2
Wrap the yarn over the hook, draw a loop through and complete the treble crochet stitch in the usual way.

Raised rib

By combining front and back post stitches, you can make a very elastic rib, ideal for cuffs on jumpers. Because the post stitches are worked into the row below, they are much shorter than standard treble crochet, so your pattern may advise a shorter turning chain, as here.

Foundation chain: Make an even number of ch + 2.
Row 1: 1 tr in fourth ch from hook, 1 tr in each ch to end, turn.
Row 2: Ch 2, skip first tr, *1 FPtr in next st, 1 BPtr in next st; rep from * to end, working last FPtr around turning chain, turn.
Repeat row 2 for pattern.

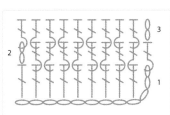

Basketweave

Combining post stitches can also be used for a basketweave effect. The woven pattern is created by working groups of front and back post stitches across the row. This stitch makes an excellent scarf, by repeating the pattern to the desired length. It can also be used for blankets and cushions. It uses a lot more yarn than standard treble crochet, but the effect is worth the investment.

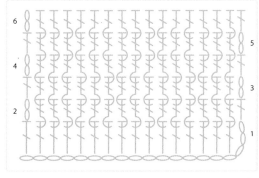

Foundation chain: Make a multiple of 6 ch + 7.
Row 1: 1 tr in fourth ch from hook, 1 tr in each ch to end, turn.
Row 2: Ch 2, skip first tr, *1 FPtr in each of next 3 sts, 1 BPtr in each of next 3 sts; rep from * to last 3 sts, 1 FPtr in each of last 3 sts, 1 tr in top of beg ch-3, turn.
Row 3: Ch 2, skip first tr, *1 BPtr in each of next 3 sts; 1 FPtr in each of next 3 sts; rep from * to last 3 sts, 1 BPtr in each of last 3 sts, 1 tr in top of beg ch-2, turn.
Row 4: Ch 2, skip first tr, *1 BPtr in each of next 3 sts, 1 FPtr in each of next 3 sts; rep from * to last 3 sts, 1 BPtr in each of last 3 sts, 1 tr in top of beg ch-2, turn.
Row 5: Ch 2, skip first tr, 1 FPtr in each of next 3 sts, 1 BPtr in each of next 3 sts; rep from * to last 3 sts, 1 FPtr in each of last 3 sts, 1 tr in top of beg ch-2, turn.
Row 6: Ch 2, skip first tr, *1 FPtr in each of next 3 sts, 1 BPtr in each of next 3 sts; rep from * to last 3 sts, 1 FPtr in each of last 3 sts, 1 tr in top of beg ch-2, turn.
Repeat rows 3–6 for pattern.

CROSSED STITCHES

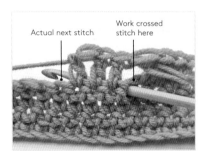

Actual next stitch   Work crossed stitch here

STEP 1
Instead of working into the next stitch in the usual way, work a crossed stitch by inserting the hook into the fabric in the place specified in the pattern. Here, the crossed stitch is worked four stitches to the right of the actual next stitch.

Bring yarn up to same height as other stitches

STEP 2
Work the stitch in the usual way, drawing the loop through the fabric up to the same height as the adjacent stitches, then continue along the row.

5 TIPS FOR ADDING TEXTURE

Liven up plain crochet patterns with extra texture, but remember that this will use up more yarn than stated in your pattern.

1 Patterns in plain treble crochet can be livened up by working panels of crossed stitches (see left). Practise the technique on a swatch first, to be sure you can match the recommended tension. A scarf would be an ideal project to try. Changes to tension would affect the overall length, but this can be rectified by working more or fewer rows. A slight difference in the width should not be too noticeable.

2 Raised treble crochets make excellent ribs for cuffs and hat brims (see page 86).

3 If a pattern calls for double crochet, try working alternate rows into front loops only and back loops only (see pages 84–85).

4 Make simple but practical washcloths in cotton yarn by working a square in double crochet, but only work into the back loops for every row. This will make a ridged cloth with plenty of stretch and visual interest (see page 84).

5 Add a row of puff stitches to the first and last rows of a plain scarf (see page 93).

Cable stitch

SPECIAL STITCH
Cable stitch: Make 1 tr, inserting hook 4 sts to the right into the last skipped dc.

Foundation chain: Make a multiple of 4 ch + 2.
Row 1 (WS): 1 dc in second ch from hook, 1 dc in each ch to end, turn.
Row 2: Ch 3 (counts as 1 tr), skip first dc, *skip next dc, 1 tr in each of next 3 dc, cable stitch; rep from * ending 1 tr in beg ch-1, turn.
Row 3: Ch 1 (counts as 1 dc), skip first tr, 1 dc in each tr across, ending 1 dc in top of beg ch-3, turn.
Repeat rows 2–3 for pattern.

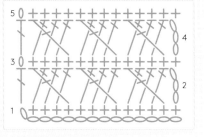

KEY
⌒ Chain
+ Double crochet
⊺ Treble crochet

SPIKE STITCHES

Also known as dropped stitches, these create a dense texture and can be worked in more than one colour to create striking stripe patterns. They are usually worked in double crochet. With spike stitches, the hook is inserted into a stitch several rows below the row you are working. You need to draw up a loop long enough to reach the height of the working row, so that it does not to squash the stitches on the rows in between. Several spike stitches can be made into one stitch and this is very effective if worked in a contrasting colour.

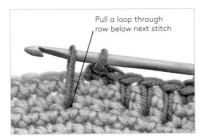

Pull a loop through row below next stitch

STEP 1
Insert the hook from front to back into the specified row below, as instructed in the pattern (here, one row below the current row). Wrap the yarn over the hook and draw a loop through. Draw the loop up the height of the row you are working on.

Don't pull spike too tight

STEP 2
Complete the stitch in the usual way, taking care not to pull the loop too tightly or the stitch will distort your work.

Spiked stripes

Worked in two colours, A and B. The colour changes every two rows. Do not cut the yarn after each colour change; carry the unused yarn up the side of the work.

SPECIAL STITCH
SPdc: Spike stitch worked in double crochet by inserting hook into next st one row below.

Foundation chain: Using A, make a multiple of 8 ch + 1.
Row 1: 1 dc in second ch from hook, 1 dc in each ch to end, turn.
Row 2: Ch 1, 1 dc in each st to end, changing to B on final yo, turn.
Row 3: Ch 1, *1 dc in each of next 3 sts, [SPdc] twice, 1 dc in each of next 3 sts; rep from * to end, turn.
Row 4: Ch 1, 1 dc in each st to end, changing to A on final yo, turn.
Row 5: Ch 1, *1 dc in each of next 3 sts, [SPdc] twice, 1 dc in each of next 3 sts; rep from * to end, turn.
Repeat rows 2–5 for pattern, ending with a row 2.

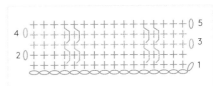

KEY
⬭ Chain
+ Double crochet
⦚ Spike double crochet

COLOUR VARIATION
Using contrasting yarn colours highlights the stitch construction and makes a busy and interesting surface pattern (above right). Changing the yarn colours to a pair that are closer to each other in tonal value produces more subtle stripes (left).

Clusters

Clusters are a striking way to add texture to crochet. At their simplest, they are groups of stitches gathered at the top or at both top and bottom. Although a number of stitches are made, the resulting cluster counts as one stitch. The three most common cluster stitches are bobbles, puffs and popcorns. Although they look slightly different from each other, interesting effects can be created by substituting one cluster for another, such as a bobble for a popcorn.

Working 4-tr cluster in chain space

BASIC CLUSTER

Groups of stitches worked into two, three or more stitches made on the previous row or directly into a chain space can be joined together at the top by leaving the last loop of each stitch on the hook, then drawing the yarn through all the loops to secure the stitch. This is exactly the same technique as an internal decrease (see pages 38–39), but it can also be used to create attractive stitch patterns. Here, 4 tr are worked together in a chain space to create an angled cluster.

Angled clusters

Rows of cluster stitches facing in different directions creates a pretty and textured fabric.

SPECIAL STITCH
CL: Cluster made of 4 tr worked together (tr4tog).

Foundation chain: Make a multiple of 5 ch + 4.
Row 1: 1 dc in fourth ch from hook, *ch 3, CL over next 4 ch, ch 1, 1 dc in next ch; rep from * to end, turn.
Row 2: Ch 5, 1 dc in first CL, *ch 3, CL in next ch-3 sp, ch 1, 1 dc in next CL; rep from * to last ch-3 sp, ch 3, CL in last ch-3 sp, ch 1, 1 tr in last dc, turn.
Row 3: Ch 1, 1 dc in first CL, *ch 3, CL in next ch-3 sp, ch 1, 1 dc in next CL; rep from * ending 1 dc in beg ch-5 sp, turn.
Repeat rows 2–3 for pattern.

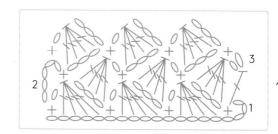

KEY
○ Chain
+ Double croche
⊤ Treble crochet
⋀ 4-tr cluster

POPCORNS

A popcorn is made by working three or more stitches into the same place, and then closing them together at the top with a chain. They stand out from the surrounding crochet fabric and almost look as if they are folded back on themselves. Popcorns are most effective made in treble crochet or longer stitches. This example is a 5-tr popcorn. If you find that your popcorns look a little floppy, you can fix this problem by working the popcorn stitch on a slightly smaller hook.

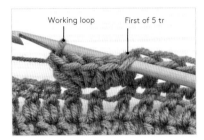

STEP 1
Work to the position of the popcorn, then work five treble crochet into the same stitch.

STEP 2
After making the fifth treble crochet, remove the hook from the working loop and insert the hook into the first stitch of the popcorn. Put the working loop back on to the hook.

STEP 3
Wrap the yarn over the hook and pull it through both the working loop and the first treble crochet of the popcorn to complete the popcorn. Continue along the row, working popcorns as required.

Popcorn columns

This highly textured stitch results in a fabric with good drape, ideal for blankets and throws.

SPECIAL STITCH
PC: Popcorn made of 5 tr.

Foundation chain: Make a multiple of 11 ch + 5.
Row 1: 1 tr in fourth ch from hook, 1 tr in next ch, *ch 2, skip next 3 ch, PC in next ch, ch 1, PC in next ch, ch 1, skip next 3 ch, 1 tr in each of next 3 ch; rep from * to end, turn.
Row 2: Ch 3 (counts as 1 tr), skip first tr, 1 tr in each of next 2 tr, *ch 3, skip next ch and PC, 2 dc in ch-1 sp between PC, ch 3, skip next PC and 2 ch, 1 tr in each of next 3 tr; rep from * to end, working last tr in top of beg ch-3, turn.
Row 3: Ch 3 (counts as 1 tr), skip first tr, 1 tr in each of next 2 tr, *ch 2, skip next 3 ch, PC in next dc, ch 1, PC in next dc, ch 1, skip next 3 ch, 1 tr in each of next 3 tr; rep from * to end, working last tr in top of beg ch-3, turn.
Repeat rows 2–3 for pattern.

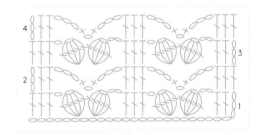

KEY
- ○ Chain
- + Double crochet
- ⊤ Treble crochet
- ⊕ 5-tr popcorn

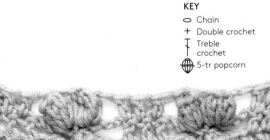

BOBBLES

A bobble is a group of stitches, usually trebles, worked into the same base stitch and then gathered together at the top. At their simplest, you can think of bobbles as multiple stitches worked as far as the last yarnover and then completed by pulling a final yarnover through all the loops on the hook. A bobble is generally worked on wrong side rows and spaced between flat stitches to bring them into relief. This example is a 4-tr bobble.

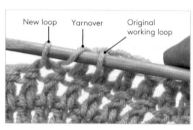

New loop Yarnover Original working loop

STEP 1
On a wrong side row, work to the position of the bobble. Wrap the yarn over the hook, insert the hook into the next stitch and pull a loop through.

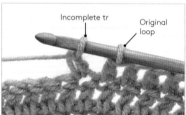

Incomplete tr Original loop

STEP 2
Wrap the yarn over the hook and pull it through the first two loops on the hook. Leave the stitch incomplete at this stage by omitting the final yarnover.

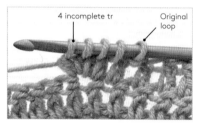

4 incomplete tr Original loop

STEP 3
Work the remaining three stitches of the bobble in the same way, leaving each stitch incomplete. You will have five loops on the hook.

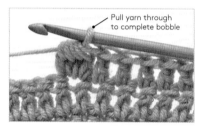

Pull yarn through to complete bobble

STEP 4
Wrap the yarn over the hook and pull it through all five loops on the hook to complete the bobble. Continue working bobbles across the row as required.

Giant bobbles

SPECIAL STITCH

BO: Bobble made of 5 tr by working [yo, insert hook into stitch and draw a loop through, yo and draw through 2 loops on hook] 5 times into same stitch, yo and draw through all 6 loops on hook.

Foundation chain: Make a multiple of 3 ch + 2.
Row 1: 1 dc in second ch from hook, 1 dc in each ch to end, turn.
Row 2: Ch 1, 1 dc in first dc, *BO in next dc, 1 dc in each of next 2 dc; rep from * to end, turn.
Row 3: Ch 1, 1 dc in each dc and BO to end, turn.
Row 4: Ch 1, 1 dc in each of first 2 dc, *BO in next dc, 1 dc in each of next 2 dc; rep from * ending last rep with 1 dc.
Row 5: As row 3.
Repeat rows 2–5 for pattern.

KEY
O Chain
+ Double crochet
⊕ 5-tr bobble

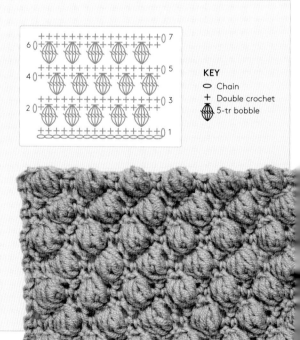

PUFFS

A puff is a number of elongated half trebles worked into the same stitch. A chain is used to close the top of the puff stitch. Any number of half trebles can be worked, and your pattern will provide this information. This example is a 5-htr puff.

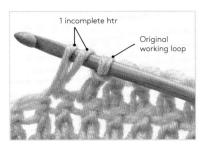

1 incomplete htr
Original working loop

STEP 1

Work to the position of the puff. Wrap the yarn over the hook, insert the hook into the stitch, wrap the yarn over the hook again and draw a loop through to the same height as the other stitches in the row. Leave the stitch incomplete at this stage by omitting the final yarnover. You will have three loops on the hook.

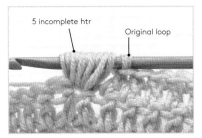

5 incomplete htr
Original loop

STEP 2

Work four more incomplete htr in the same way. You will now have 11 loops on the hook – the original loop plus two loops per htr.

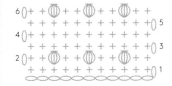

Pull yarn through all loops

STEP 3

Wrap the yarn over the hook and draw it through all of the loops on the hook.

Ch 1 to complete puff stitch

STEP 4

Make one chain to complete the puff and close the top of the stitch. Continue along the row, working puff stitches as required.

CLINIC
PUFF STITCHES ARE REALLY DIFFICULT. HOW CAN I MAKE THEM EASIER?

Many beginners find it difficult to get all their loops of an even length, as well as to work with so many loops on the hook at the same time. It can take a bit of practice to make puff stitches an even size, so always work a swatch before attempting the puff stitch in your pattern. Try making puffs with fewer loops until you get the hang of them. Make each loop long enough to move easily on the hook, so you can slip them over the hook.

Puff stitch stripes

SPECIAL STITCH
PS: Puff stitch made of 5 htr by working [yo, insert hook into stitch and draw through a loop] 5 times into same stitch, yo and draw through all 11 loops on hook, ch 1.

Foundation chain: Make a multiple of 3 ch + 3.
Row 1: 1 dc into second ch from hook, 1 dc in each ch to end, turn.
Row 2: Ch 1, 1 dc in each of first 2 dc, *PS in next dc, 1 dc in each of next 2 dc; rep from * to end, turn.
Rows 3–5: Ch 1, 1 dc in each dc and PS to end, turn.
Repeat rows 2–5 for pattern, ending with a row 3.

KEY
○ Chain
⊤ Treble crochet
🮲 5-htr puff stitch

Mesh and filet

Mesh and openwork stitches are a very simple way to crochet because the fabric is mostly made up of large areas of chain. Lightweight and easy to memorise, mesh crochet is ideal for summer scarves, wraps and openwork garments. Derived from the French for net, filet is characterised by an open mesh background with a pattern or motif picked out in solid blocks of stitches.

3 **YARNS FOR MESH AND FILET CROCHET**

1 A mesh or trellis pattern worked in a smooth yarn or fine cotton will create a fabric that is light and easy to wear, yet heavy enough to drape around the neck for a scarf.

2 For more of a challenge, try a mohair yarn. The fine fibres are often difficult to crochet, but the combination of treble crochet and chains can result in a stunning and luxurious wrap.

3 Generally worked in a fine cotton, filet can also be made in heavier yarns, although the pattern may not be so clear. Make sure you choose a smooth yarn in a plain colour to practise.

MESH AND TRELLIS

These are the simplest form of lace stitches and are created from lengths of chain anchored with stitches. Mesh patterns are created from a regular grid of chains and stitches. Patterns with longer chain spaces, which allows them to curve upwards to form arches, are known as trellis patterns. For both types, an accurate foundation chain is essential, and you may find it helpful to insert a stitch marker in every 20th chain so that you don't lose count.

CLASSIC MESH

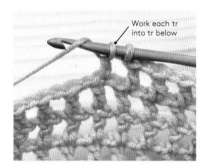
Work each tr into tr below

The classic mesh pattern is a series of alternating chains and treble crochet stitches. Work each treble crochet into the treble crochet made on the previous row to form a regular grid of chain spaces.

OFFSET MESH

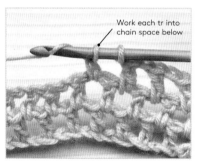
Work each tr into chain space below

STEP 1
To create an offset mesh pattern, work each treble crochet stitch into a chain space on the row below to form a grid of alternating chain spaces.

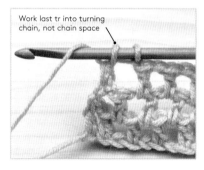
Work last tr into turning chain, not chain space

STEP 2
Work the final stitch of the row into the top of the turning chain, not into the last chain space. This creates a firmer and neater edge to the crochet fabric.

Work 1 dc into chain space to anchor trellis

TRELLIS

The delicate arches of the trellis stitch are created by anchoring lengths of chain to the chain spaces on the previous row with a double crochet stitch. Insert the hook into the chain space and complete the double crochet in the usual way.

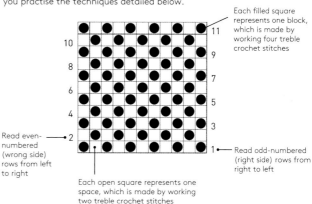

FILET CROCHET

Filet is made from a regular square mesh, with some of the holes in the mesh filled in with treble crochet stitches to form a design or repeating pattern. A written pattern for filet crochet can look very complicated, with a large number of instructions and abbreviations, so charts are used for brevity. Once you understand how they work, they make filet much simpler.

Block Space

WORKING FROM A FILET CHART

Filet charts are numbered at the sides and you should follow the numbered sequence of rows upwards from the bottom of the chart, working from side to side. The squares on the chart that are filled in or have a dot or cross at the centre are called blocks; the empty squares are called spaces. The spaces represent areas of open mesh, while the blocks indicate where stitches should be made. Generally, filet is composed of a regular grid of treble crochet stitches. A filet crochet unit comprises a beginning treble crochet, either two chains for a space or two treble crochet stitches for a block and an ending treble crochet. The ending treble crochet stitch is also the beginning treble crochet of the next filet unit.

SIMPLE CHEQUERBOARD
This is the most simple filet chart and will help you practise the techniques detailed below.

Each filled square represents one block, which is made by working four treble crochet stitches

Read even-numbered (wrong side) rows from left to right

Read odd-numbered (right side) rows from right to left

Each open square represents one space, which is made by working two treble crochet stitches separated by two chains

MAKING THE FOUNDATION CHAIN
Filet charts begin with the first row, so you will need to calculate the number of chains required for the foundation chain unless there is also a written pattern that provides this information. Count the number of squares across the row (or stitch repeat) and multiply by three, then add one extra chain. For example, for a chart of 10 squares, you will need to make 31 chains (10 x 3 + 1). A turning chain is also needed – add four turning chains if the first square is a space; add two turning chains if the first square is a block.

STARTING THE FIRST ROW WITH A SPACE

1 tr being worked

8th chain from hook

Work the first treble crochet stitch into the eighth chain from the hook to form the first space. Continue along the row, working spaces and blocks as they appear on the chart.

STARTING THE FIRST ROW WITH A BLOCK

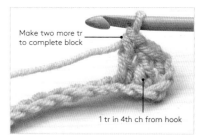

Make two more tr to complete block

1 tr in 4th ch from hook

Work the first treble crochet stitch into the fourth chain from the hook; the skipped three chains count as the first treble. Then make one treble in each of the next two chains to complete the first block. Continue along the row.

WORKING A SPACE OVER A BLOCK

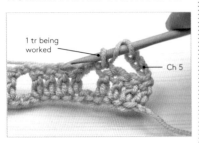

STEP 1

At the beginning of a row, make five chains (counts as 1 tr, ch 2), skip the first three stitches and make one treble in the next stitch.

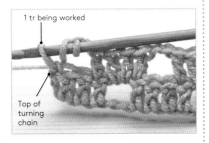

STEP 2

At the end of a row, work to the last four trebles. Make one treble in the next stitch, make two chains, skip two stitches and make the last treble into the top of the turning chain.

WORKING A SPACE OVER A SPACE

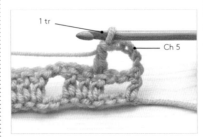

STEP 1

At the beginning of a row, make five chains (counts as 1 tr, ch 2), then skip the first stitch and the next two chains, and make one treble in the next stitch.

STEP 2

At the end of a row, make one treble in the last stitch of the row, make two chains, skip the next two chains and make the last treble into the top of the turning chain.

WORKING A BLOCK OVER A BLOCK

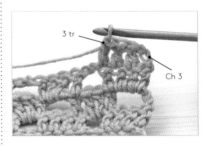

STEP 1

At the beginning of a row, make three chains (counts as 1 tr), skip the first stitch, then work one treble in each of next three stitches to complete the block.

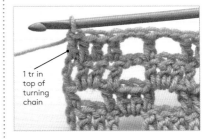

STEP 2

At the end of a row, finish by making one treble in each of last three trebles and one treble into the top of the turning chain.

CHAIN SPACE VARIATION

When working a block over a space, you can either work the trebles into the chain space as shown in the step photographs on the right, or work them into the chain stitches as shown below. The important thing is to be consistent.

WORKING A BLOCK OVER A SPACE

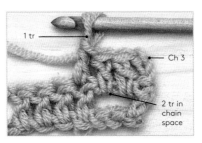

STEP 1

At the beginning of a row, make three chains (counts as 1 tr), skip the first stitch, make two trebles in the next chain space and then one treble in the next stitch.

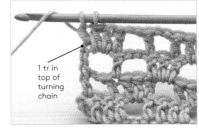

STEP 2

At the end of a row, make one treble in the last treble, two trebles in the next chain space and then one treble into the top of the turning chain.

Classic mesh

Foundation chain: Make an odd number of ch + 5.
Row 1: 1 tr in sixth ch from hook, *ch 1, skip next ch, 1 tr in next ch; rep from * to end, turn.
Row 2: Ch 4 (counts as 1 tr, ch 1), *1 tr in next tr, ch 1; rep from * to end, working last tr in 4th ch of beg ch-5, turn.
Row 3: Ch 4 (counts as 1 tr, ch 1), *1 tr in next tr, ch 1; rep from * to end, working last tr in 3rd ch of beg ch-4, turn.
Repeat row 3 for pattern.

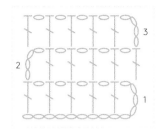

KEY
○ Chain
⊤ Treble crochet

Arched trellis

Foundation chain: Make a multiple of 4 ch + 2.
Row 1: 1 dc in sixth ch from hook, *ch 5, skip next 3 ch, 1 dc in next ch; rep from * to end, turn.
Row 2: *Ch 5, 1 dc in next ch-5 sp; rep from * to end, turn.
Repeat row 2 for pattern.

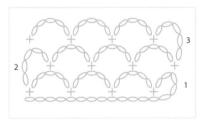

KEY
○ Chain
+ Double crochet

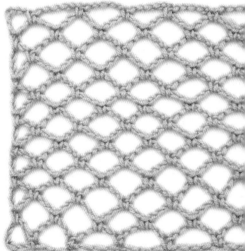

Little crosses filet

Sometimes called little flowers, this classic filet pattern has spaces and blocks at intervals to create an open mesh with small filled areas resembling crosses or flower petals. See page 95 for how to read a filet chart. To work one repeat of this chart, you will need to start with a foundation of 38 chains.

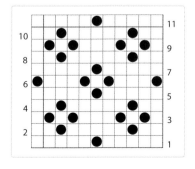

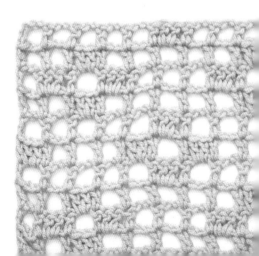

Chevrons and waves

Chevron and wave patterns are created by working a series of paired increases and decreases to create the familiar rickrack or zigzag effects most commonly seen on brightly coloured blankets. Regular increases create peaks and regular decreases create troughs, which results in an attractive stripe effect that is most noticeable when worked in different colours. Chevron patterns can be used to create gentle waves or sharply angled stripes.

CLINIC

WHAT'S THE DIFFERENCE BETWEEN A CHEVRON AND A WAVE?

Patterns with sharp points are generally called chevrons and gentler patterns are called waves. Both techniques usually begin with a set-up row, which sets the position of the increases and decreases. The pattern is then repeated over one or two rows, making it fairly simple to memorise. If you are working in many colours, try to work an even number of rows in each colour, so that all the ends can be woven in on the same side.

SHARP CHEVRON

3-dc peak

Skipped stitch forms trough

STEP 1
Work multiple stitches into the same place, as instructed in the pattern. This increase forms the peaks of the chevron. Here, three double crochet are worked into the same stitch to form a crisp, pointed peak.

STEP 2
Form troughs by working the decrease as instructed in the pattern. Here, a stitch is skipped to create the decrease. Once you understand the principle of pairing increases and decreases, you can follow any of the chevron patterns that are widely available.

SOFT WAVE

3 tr in same stitch

Tr3tog

3 tr in centre tr of previous 3-tr group

STEP 1
Working the peaks and troughs in treble crochet produces a softer wave pattern than double crochet. In this example, the increase for the peak is worked by making three trebles in the same stitch.

STEP 2
The troughs are formed by working tr3tog to decrease by two stitches. Again, this produces a gentler wave pattern than skipping a stitch to form the trough.

STEP 3
On the next row, the increases for the peaks are worked into the centre treble crochet stitch of the 3-tr peak of the previous row.

Sharp chevron

Worked in two colours, A and B.

Foundation chain: Using A, make a multiple of 16 ch + 2.
Row 1: 2 dc in second ch from hook, *1 dc in each of next 7 ch, skip next ch, 1 dc in each of next
7 ch, 3 dc in next ch; rep from * ending 2 dc in last ch and changing to B on final yo, turn.
Row 2: Ch 1, 2 dc in first dc, *1 dc in each of next 7 dc, skip next 2 dc, 1 dc in each of next 7 dc, 3 dc in next dc; rep from * ending 2 dc in last dc and changing to A on final yo, turn.
Repeat row 2 for pattern, alternating A and B.

Soft wave

Foundation chain: Make a multiple of 10 ch + 4.
Row 1: 1 tr in fourth ch from hook, *1 tr in each of next 3 ch, tr3tog over next 3 ch, 1 tr in each of next 3 ch, 3 tr in next ch; rep from * ending 2 tr in last ch.
Row 2: Ch 3 (counts as 1 tr), 1 tr in same place, *1 tr in each of next 3 tr, tr3tog over next 3 tr, 1 tr in each of next 3 tr, 3 tr in next tr, rep from * ending 2 tr in top of beg ch-3.
Repeat row 2 for pattern.

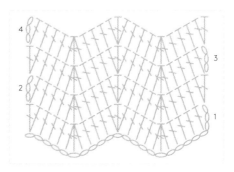

KEY
⊶ Chain
+ Double crochet

KEY
⊶ Chain
T Treble crochet
A Treble crochet 3 together

Shells and fans

These are formed from a group of three or more stitches that share the same stitch or chain space, causing the characteristic shell or fan shape. Shells can be worked above each other or interlocked by working into the spaces between each shell. They are usually worked with an odd number of stitches so that there is a centre stitch. Each stitch that makes up the shell or fan counts as a stitch. Often stitches are skipped on either side to allow for the extra width at the top. Shells and fans are often combined with chain spaces to create lacy stitch patterns.

BASIC SHELL

5 tr into same chain

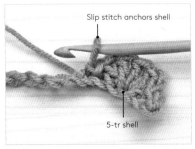

Slip stitch anchors shell

5-tr shell

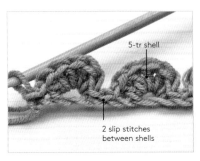

5-tr shell

2 slip stitches between shells

STEP 1
Make the required length of foundation chain using a size larger hook to give you plenty of room for working the shells. Switch back to your usual hook. Work as instructed to the position of the shell, then work the shell stitches into the same chain. This example is a 5-tr shell.

STEP 2
Continue to the position of the next shell as instructed. Here, one slip stitch is worked into each of the next two chains. Working multiple trebles into the same chain creates the distinctive shell shape, while slip stitches on either side allow enough room for the shell to spread.

STEP 3
Continue to the end of the row, working five trebles in the next stitch, then one slip stitch in each of the next two chains.

LACY SHELL

Work shell into dc below

Anchor shell with 1 dc in chain space

STEP 1
Separating the shells with chain spaces produces an attractive lacy fabric. Here, rows of 5-tr shells are alternated with rows of chains anchored to the top of each shell with a double crochet stitch. Each shell is worked into this double crochet stitch.

STEP 2
A double crochet is worked into the chain space to anchor the shell. This allows the shell to spread and raises the centre of the chain loops, so that the chain spaces echo the shape of the shells.

CLINIC

WHAT'S THE DIFFERENCE BETWEEN A FAN AND A SHELL?

The terms shell and fan are often used interchangeably by designers. In general, shell patterns are normally made across one row, while a fan pattern can take more than one row to complete and is often based on a row of chain stitches to make the crochet stitches fan out more. When working shell patterns, it can help to make the foundation chain using a slightly bigger hook, so that each chain has enough space to work multiple stitches into.

Lacy shells

Foundation chain: Make a multiple of 6 ch + 1.
Row 1: 1 dc in second ch from hook, *skip next 2 ch, 5 tr in next ch (shell made), skip next 2 ch, 1 dc in next ch; rep from * to end, turn.
Row 2: *Ch 5, 1 dc in centre tr of next shell; rep from * to last dc, ch 2, 1 tr in last dc, turn.
Row 3: Ch 1, 1 dc in first tr, *5 tr in next dc, 1 dc in next ch-5 sp; rep from * ending 1 dc in 3rd ch of beg ch-5.
Repeat rows 2–3 for pattern.

KEY
◯ Chain
✛ Double crochet
T Treble crochet

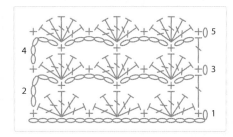

Solid shells

Foundation chain: Make a multiple of 6 ch + 2.
Row 1: 1 dc in second ch from hook, *skip next 2 ch, 5 tr in next ch (shell made), skip next 2 ch, 1 dc in next ch; rep from * to end, turn.
Row 2: Ch 3 (counts as 1 tr), 2 tr in same place (half shell made), *skip next 2 tr, 1 dc in next tr, skip next 2 tr, 5 tr in next dc; rep from * ending 3 tr in last dc, turn.
Row 3: Ch 1, 1 dc in first tr, *skip next 2 tr, 5 tr in next dc, skip next 2 tr, 1 dc in next tr; rep from * ending 1 dc in top of beg ch-3, turn.
Repeat rows 2–3 for pattern.

KEY
◯ Chain
✛ Double crochet
T Treble crochet

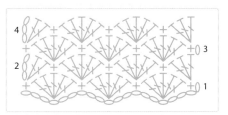

FAN STITCH

This simple fan pattern is made by working seven treble crochet stitches into a chain space. This allows the trebles to fan out. In this example, the fans are combined with a trellis pattern (see page 94) to create an open, lacy fabric.

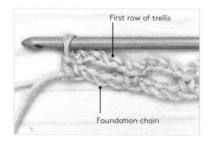

First row of trellis

Foundation chain

STEP 1
Work to the end of row 1 of the fan and trellis pattern (see below). This creates a trellis of chains anchored at regular intervals to the foundation chain.

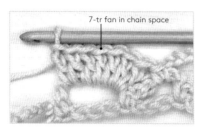

7-tr fan in chain space

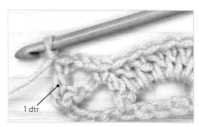

1 dtr

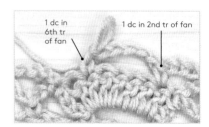

1 dc in 6th tr of fan

1 dc in 2nd tr of fan

STEP 2
On the next row, fans are alternated with areas of trellis. To work a fan, insert the hook into the chain space and work the number of stitches required (here, 7 tr). The stitches will fan out over the length of the chain.

STEP 3
To balance the pattern at the end of the row, work a double treble crochet into the last double crochet of the previous row. This brings the final length of chain up to the height of the centre of the fan.

STEP 4
Work another row of trellis only, anchoring the lengths of chain to the centre of each chain space, and to the second and sixth stitch of each fan. Continue alternating rows of trellis and fans as required.

Fan and trellis

Foundation chain: Make a multiple of 12 ch.
Row 1: 1 dc in second ch from hook, *ch 5, skip next 3 ch, 1 dc in next ch; rep from * to last 2 ch, ch 2, skip next ch, 1 tr in last ch, turn.
Row 2: Ch 1, 1 dc in first tr, skip next 2 ch, *7 tr in next ch-5 sp, 1 dc in next ch-5 sp**, ch 5, 1 dc in next ch-5 sp; rep from * ending last rep at **, ch 2, 1 dtr in last dc, turn.
Row 3: Ch 1, 1 dc in first dtr, *ch 5, 1 dc in second tr of next fan, ch 5, 1 dc in sixth tr of same fan**, ch 5, 1 dc in next ch-5 sp; rep from * ending last rep at **, ch 2, 1 dtr in last dc, turn.
Repeat rows 2–3 for pattern.

KEY
◯ Chain
+ Double crochet
⊤ Treble crochet
⊤ Double treble crochet

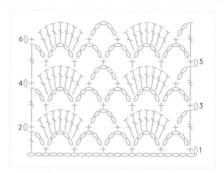

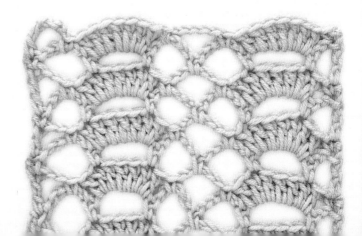

Three-dimensional texture

The ability to create three-dimensional stitches has played a role in crochet's recent popularity with fashion designers. Here are three stitches that use standard techniques but in a different way than usual to create 3D texture. Note that these stitches use more yarn than traditional stitches and this can add to the weight of the finished item.

CROCHET RUFFLE

If you like the idea of adding some texture and visual interest to your project, but don't feel ready to tackle these stitches, a simple crochet ruffle can be very effective. This ruffle is made by working three trebles into each double crochet stitch.

ASTRAKHAN STITCH

This stitch is highly textured and is ideal as an edging on collars and cuffs. Also known as chain loop stitch, it is based on working multiple chains to create loops on right side rows. This example is worked on a background of treble crochet.

Ch 7

Join with slip stitch in front loop

Slip stitch in both loops of turning chain

Unworked loop of row 1

Chain loops on RS

STEP 1
Start with a row of standard treble crochet, then turn the work to begin the first chain loop row. Make the first chain loop (here, ch 7) and then work a slip stitch into the front loop only of the next treble crochet.

STEP 2
Continue along the row, making a series of chain loops followed by a slip stitch into the front loop of the next treble. Finish with a slip stitch through both loops of the top of the turning chain.

STEP 3
Turn and work a row of treble crochet, working each stitch into the unworked loops of the first row of treble crochet. Continue alternating rows of chain loops and trebles in this way.

Astrakhan stitch

Foundation chain: Make any number of ch + 3.
Row 1 (WS): 1 tr in fourth ch from hook, 1 tr in each ch to end, turn.
Row 2: *Ch 7, sl st through front loop of next tr; rep from * ending sl st in both loops of top of beg ch-3, turn.
Row 3: Ch 3 (counts as 1 tr), *1 tr in unworked loop of next tr on row 1; rep from * to end, turn.
Repeat rows 2–3 for pattern.

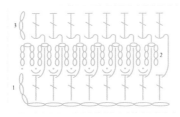

KEY
⌒ Chain
• Slip stitch
T Treble crochet
⌣ Through front loop

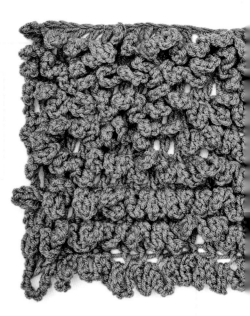

LOOP STITCH

In this simple stitch, lengths of yarn are looped around a finger. It makes an ideal trim for a scarf or garment. Loop stitches are usually worked on wrong side rows.

Loop yarn around finger

Pull both ends of loop through stitch

STEP 1

Insert the hook into the next stitch. Pull up the working yarn on your finger to form a loop. You can vary the size of the loop as you wish.

STEP 2

Use the hook to draw both strands of the loop through the stitch. Remove your finger, wrap the yarn over the hook and draw it through all three loops on the hook to complete the loop stitch.

Banded loop stitch

Foundation chain: Make a multiple of 8 ch + 2.
Row 1: 1 tr in fourth ch from hook, 1 tr in each ch to end, turn.
Row 2: Ch 1, 1 dc in each of first 2 tr, *work loop stitch in each of next 4 tr, 1 dc in each of next 4 tr; rep from * ending 1 dc in last tr, 1 dc in top of beg ch-3, turn.
Row 3: Ch 3 (counts as 1 tr), skip first dc, 1 tr in each st to end, turn.
Repeat rows 2–3 for pattern.

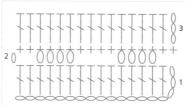

KEY

○ Chain
+ Double crochet
Ⴕ Treble crochet
Ö Loop stitch

CROCODILE STITCH

Crocodile stitch is a recent phenomenon and there are many variations. It can be tricky to manipulate the hook and the yarn, but it is worth persevering. A basic crocodile stitch involves working multiple stitches around the posts of a pair of treble crochet to create a highly textured effect that looks a little bit like petals or scales (hence the name). Rows of crocodile stitch are alternated with rows of paired trebles.

Post of first tr of pair

STEP 1

Work a row of paired treble crochet stitches separated by chains (as row 1 of the pattern opposite). The first half of the crocodile stitch will be worked around the post of the first treble of the pair, with the hook inserted under the post from right to left, as shown.

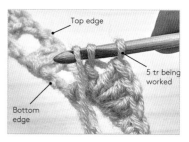

Top edge

5 tr being worked

Bottom edge

STEP 2

Work the required number of trebles around this first post (here, 5 tr), starting at the top of the post and working down to the bottom. To make it easier to work the stitches, turn the work 90 degrees clockwise, so that the post you are working around is horizontal in front of you, with the top edge of the crochet to the right.

First half of crocodile stitch

Bottom edge

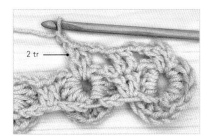

2 tr

STEP 3
Turn the work the right way up again. After completing the first half of the crocodile stitch, the hook and working loop will be at the bottom of the crochet.

STEP 6
Turn the work and work another row of paired trebles. To work a paired treble above a crocodile stitch, insert the hook into the space at the centre of the crocodile stitch.

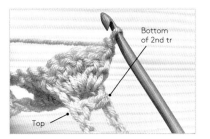

Bottom of 2nd tr

Top

STEP 4
Make one chain, and then turn the work 90 degrees anticlockwise, so that the post of the second treble is horizontal in front of you, with the top edge of the crochet to the left. Work another 5 tr around this post, starting at the bottom of the post and working up to the top.

Crocodile stitch

SPECIAL STITCH
CS: Crocodile stitch made of 5 tr around post of first tr working from top to bottom of tr, ch 1, 5 tr around post of next tr working from bottom to top of tr.

Foundation chain: Make a multiple of 3 ch + 1.
Row 1 (WS): 1 tr in fourth ch from hook, *ch 2, skip next 2 ch, 2 tr in next ch; rep from * to end, turn.
Row 2: Ch 1, CS around first tr pair, *ch 1, skip next tr pair, CS around next tr pair; rep from * to end, turn.
Row 3: Sl st into centre of first CS, ch 3 (counts as 1 tr), 1 tr in same place, *ch 2, 1 tr in each of 2 skipped tr, ch 2, 2 tr in next CS; rep from * to end, turn.
Row 4: Ch 1, skip first tr pair, CS around next tr pair, *ch 1, skip next tr pair, CS around next tr pair; rep from * to last tr pair, sl st in top of beg ch-3, turn.
Row 5: Ch 3, 1 tr in top of next tr (counts as first tr pair), *ch 2, 2 tr in centre of next CS, ch 2, 1 tr in each of 2 skipped tr; rep from * to end, turn.
Repeat rows 2–5 for pattern.

Ch 1

STEP 5
If you turn the work the right way up again, you can see the completed crocodile stitch. Make one chain and then continue working crocodile stitches to the end of the row as instructed in the pattern.

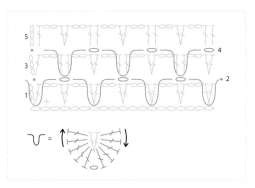

KEY
⌒ Chain
• Slip stitch
╪ Treble crochet
⋎ Crocodile stitch

Colourwork

Intarsia and tapestry crochet are more challenging techniques, but are very rewarding ways to introduce colour into your crochet. They are generally worked in double crochet, with colour changes made on the final yarnover of the preceding stitch using the incomplete stitch method (see page 32). Both are worked from a chart indicating which colour is to be used where, and each square on the chart represents one stitch.

TAPESTRY CROCHET

Also known as jacquard crochet, this technique involves using more than one colour across the row, with the unworked colour being carried behind the row and enclosed along the back of the work (as when working over yarn tails when joining in a new yarn). Double crochet is most commonly used because it is the stitch that most effectively traps the unworked yarn as you travel across the row. With taller stitches, you must be careful to hold the unused colour in place so that it does not show through on the right side.

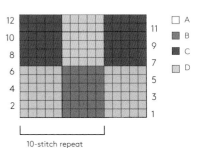

□ A
■ B
■ C
□ D

10-stitch repeat

TAPESTRY CHECKS

This example uses four colours of yarn (A, B, C, D) but is worked using only two colours at a time. You begin with a foundation chain, so count the number of squares on the chart. This example is worked over a multiple of 10 chains, plus 5 chains to balance the pattern, plus 1 turning chain for double crochet.

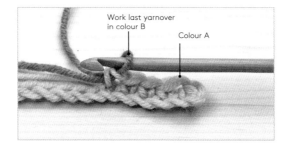

Work last yarnover in colour B

Colour A

STEP 1
Using A, work the first four double crochet stitches of the first row. Work another double crochet, but this time change to the second colour (B) on the final yarnover.

Work last yarnover in colour A

STEP 2
Using B, work the next five double crochet stitches, carrying A across the back of the work and enclosing it as you go. Change to A on the final yarnover of the fifth stitch.

Enclose yarn A within B stitches at back of work

STEP 3
Continue to work across the chart, changing colours where indicated. Here, you can see the unused colour (A) being enclosed within the B stitches.

Unused A enclosed within B stitches

STEP 4
If you look closely at the wrong side of the work, you can see the unused yarn neatly enclosed within the crochet stitches.

INTARSIA CROCHET

Intarsia can be used to create blocks of colour or pictures in your crochet. Instead of carrying the unused yarn across the back of each row as you would in tapestry crochet, a separate ball or bobbin of yarn is wound for each separate area of colour. It is best to wind the yarn before starting the project. How much yarn to wind is a matter of judgement and you should be guided by how big each area of colour is. The pattern will usually tell you how big to make the foundation chain. When you are following the chart, remember to make the appropriate turning chain (one chain for double crochet) and count your stitches after each row.

INTARSIA SQUARES

This block is worked entirely in double crochet and uses three colours (A, B, C). You will need to wind two balls of the background colour (A) – one each for working the background on each side of the central design – plus one ball of each colour for the central motif design (B, C).

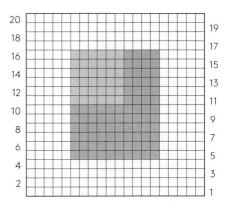

☐ A
▨ B
☐ C

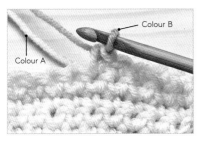

STEP 1
Follow the chart until the stitch before you need to change colour for the first time (row 5 in this example, which is a right side row). Work the first yarnover in the background colour (A). Complete the stitch in the first motif colour (B), leaving the new yarn tail and old colour on the wrong side of the work.

STEP 2
Continue using the motif colour until one stitch before the background colour is required again. Work the first yarnover in the motif colour, then complete the stitch using a second ball of the background colour. Drop the motif colour and leave it at the wrong side of the work. Continue to the end of the row.

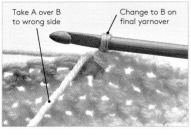

STEP 3
Turn and work the next row of the chart (here, row 6, a wrong side row) until one stitch before the next colour change. Use the new colour (B) for the final yarnover of this stitch, then bring the old colour (A) over the top of the new colour to the wrong side of the work. This prevents a gap where the colour change happens.

STEP 4
At the end of the wrong side row, all the yarn tails should be positioned on the wrong side of the work, ready to work the next row.

STEP 5
To work rows with the right side facing you, all yarns will be at the back of the work. As you change colour, leave the old yarn (A) at the back ready for the next row, and wrap the new colour (B) around and over the old colour to work the final yarnover. This will prevent gaps at the colour change.

Quick
start
project:

Child's shell stitch bag

This pretty bag is perfect for a little girl, but you can easily make it suitable for an adult by working a longer strap to wear it over the shoulder or across the body. The shell pattern repeat is simple to memorise and the colour changes add extra interest.

FINISHED SIZE
Bag: 21 x 21cm (8¼ x 8¼in)
Strap: 60cm (23½in); adjustable

TENSION
3½ shells and 11 rows = 10cm (4in) square over shell pattern

YOU WILL NEED
• 1 x 50g ball of DK-weight wool yarn in each of orange (A), yellow (B) and green (C); Tracey used DMC Woolly, 100% merino wool with approx. 125m (136yd) per ball, in 102 (A), 093 (B) and 081 (C), but any DK yarn can be substituted
• 4mm crochet hook
• Yarn needle

ABBREVIATIONS AND TECHNIQUES
ch = chain (page 18)
dc = double crochet (page 23)
RS = right side
sl st = slip stitch (page 22)
st(s) = stitch(es)
tr = treble crochet (page 25)
WS = wrong side
Joining yarn (page 32)
Shells (pages 100–101)
Double crochet seam (page 45)
Working into one loop (page 84)
Backstitch (page 43)

PATTERN NOTES
• This bag is made using the solid shells pattern on page 101 using three alternating colours. Change colours on the final yarnover of the last stitch on each row. There is no need to cut the yarn; the correct colour of yarn will be waiting for you at the end of each row.
• When edging the front and back, make sure that the stitch counts for both pieces are the same because this will help when joining them together. When joining the two pieces, note that no extra stitches are worked at the corners. This creates the curved corners at the base of the bag.
• Ch 1 at the beginning of a row or round does not count as a stitch.
• You could easily line the bag with a pretty fabric if you wish. Use the crocheted front and back to make a paper template, then cut out two pieces of fabric and sew them together, leaving the top open. Remember to leave a seam allowance! Hem around the top, then insert the lining into the bag with RS facing inwards and hand sew the top of the lining to the crochet fabric.

FRONT AND BACK (ALIKE)

Foundation chain: Using A, ch 38.
Follow the solid shells pattern in the following colour sequence:

Row 1: Yarn A.
Row 2: Yarn B.
Row 3: Yarn C.
Rows 4–21: As rows 1–3.
Row 22: Yarn A.
Fasten off and weave in ends.

EDGING FRONT AND BACK

Edge each piece separately as follows.
Row 1: With RS facing, join A with sl st to top left-hand edge (row 22), 1 dc in same place as sl st, then work 1 dc in last st of each row to bottom left-hand corner, turn 90 degrees, then working into the underside of foundation ch work 3 dc in first ch, 1 dc in each ch to end, 3 dc in last ch, turn 90 degrees, work 1 dc in last st of each row to top right-hand edge.
Fasten off and weave in ends.

JOINING FRONT AND BACK

Row 1: With WS together and working through both layers of fabric, join A with sl st to first dc at top left-hand edge, 1 dc in same place as sl st, then work 1 dc in each st to top right-hand edge.
Fasten off and weave in ends.

STRAP

Foundation chain: Using C, ch 5.
Row 1: 1 dc in second ch from hook, 1 dc in each ch to end, turn.
Row 2: Ch 1, 1 dc in each dc to end, turn.
Rows 3–90: As row 2.
To make a longer strap, repeat row 2 to length required.
Fasten off and weave in ends.

EDGING THE STRAP

Round 1: Join A with sl st to last dc of last row, ch 1, turn 90 degrees, work 1 dc in last st of each row to foundation ch, turn 90 degrees, work 1 dc into underside of each foundation ch, turn 90 degrees, work 1 dc in last st of each row to top, turn 90 degrees, work 1 dc in each dc of final row, do not turn and do not join.
Round 2: Sl sl through back loop of each st around, join with sl st to last dc.
Fasten off and weave in ends.

JOINING THE STRAP

To attach strap to bag, align short edges of strap along top of bag, centred on side seam, and sew into place with backstitch.

Guest Designer Maaike van Koert

My name is Maaike, a Dutch girl who lives with her husband, baby girl and chocolate Lab in a pretty village in the south of The Netherlands. We moved to Toronto, Canada, in 2011 for two years. During that time I worked on my first crochet designs and loved it so much that I just couldn't stop. Travels in North America were my inspiration; new colour combinations turned straight into striped baby blanket designs. After returning to The Netherlands, my first crochet book *Puur Haken* was launched in the summer of 2014. You can find my designs online through www.creJJtion.com, as well as creJJtion on Etsy and Ravelry.

Popcorn purses

These cute little purses allow you to try out popcorn stitches as the centre of a beautiful textured flower. Spike stitches are used to define an extra layer of petals around the popcorn centre. Add leaves and a scalloped edging for extra detail if you wish. A small project like a purse is quick to make and would be perfect as a gift.

FINISHED SIZE
Small: 7.5cm (3in) diameter
Large: 10cm (4in) diameter

TENSION
Make first side of purse and check against stated dimensions; adjust hook size if necessary to match required diameter (see also pattern notes). Note that this project does not need to be blocked

YOU WILL NEED
• 1 x 50g ball of 4ply-weight cotton yarn in each of pink or apricot (A), cream (B), light or dark blue (C) and green (D); Maaike chose Catania 100% Cotton, with approx. 125m (137yd) per ball, in Light Pink 246 (A), Natural 105 (B), Aqua 397 (C) and Lime 392 (D) for the small purse, and Apricot 263 (A), Natural 105 (B), Mallard 400 (C) and Lime 392 (D) for the large purse, but any 4ply yarn can be substituted

• 3mm crochet hook
• Yarn needle
• Sew-on semicircular metal coin purse frame: 7.5cm (3in) diameter for small purse; 10cm (4in) diameter for large purse

ABBREVIATIONS AND TECHNIQUES
beg PC = beginning popcorn made of ch 3 (counts as 1 tr), 3 tr (page 91)
ch = chain (page 18)
dc = double crochet (page 23)
htr = half treble crochet (page 24)
PC = popcorn made of 4 tr (page 91)
RS = right side
sl st = slip stitch (page 22)
SPdc = spike double crochet worked into next st one round below (page 89)
st(s) = stitch(es)
tr = treble crochet (page 25)
Starting the round (page 56)
Joining yarn (page 32)
Double crochet seam (page 45)

PATTERN NOTES
• Tight stitches are required to make this purse nice and firm; if your tension is loose, try a smaller hook size.
• You can adjust the size of the purse to suit your purse frame by working more or fewer rounds in yarn C as required.
• Ch 1 at the beginning of dc rounds or rows does not count as a stitch. Ch 2 at the beginning counts as 1 htr; ch 3 at the beginning counts as 1 tr.
• The larger purse is shown with an optional scalloped edging. This is worked directly on to the finished purse. The clinic opposite shows how to work the edging on to the purse, but see also page 122 for more about this type of edging in general.

FRONT AND BACK (ALIKE)

Foundation ring: Using A, ch 3 and join with sl st to form a ring.

Round 1: Ch 1, 6 dc into ring, join with sl st to first dc. (6 dc)

Round 2: Beg PC in first dc, [ch 2, PC in next dc] 5 times, ch 2, join with sl st to top of beg PC. (6 popcorns and 6 ch sp)

Round 3: Sl st into next ch-2 sp, (beg PC, ch 2, PC) in same place, [(ch 2, PC, ch 2, PC) in next ch-2 sp] 5 times, ch 2, join with sl st to top of beg PC. (12 popcorns and 12 ch sp)

Fasten off A and join B to any ch-2 sp.

Round 4: Ch 1, 3 dc in same place, [3 dc in next ch-2 sp] 11 times, join with sl st to first dc. (36 dc)

Round 5: Ch 1, 1 dc in each of first 3 dc, 2 dc in next dc, [1 dc in each of next 3 dc, 2 dc in next dc] 8 times, join with sl st to first dc. (45 dc)

Round 6: Ch 1, 1 dc in each of first 4 dc, 2 dc in next dc, [1 dc in each of next 4 dc, 2 dc in next dc] 8 times, join with sl st to first dc. (54 dc)

Change to C.

Round 7: Ch 1, 1 dc in each of first 4 dc, *SPdc in next dc, 2 dc in next dc, 1 dc in each of next 4 dc; rep from * to last 2 dc, SPdc in next dc, 2 dc in last dc, join with sl st to first dc. (63 dc)

Small purse only:

Round 8: Ch 1, 1 dc in each dc around, join with sl st to first dc.

Fasten off and weave in ends.

Large purse only:

Round 8: Ch 2, skip first dc, 1 htr in each st around, join with sl st to top of beg ch-2. (63 htr)

Round 9: As round 8.

Fasten off and weave in ends.

LEAVES (MAKE 4 PER PURSE)

Using D, ch 5, 1 dc in second ch from hook, 1 htr in next ch, 1 tr in each of next 2 ch.

Fasten off, leaving a 15cm (6in) tail for sewing to flower.

TO ASSEMBLE THE PURSE

Using a yarn needle, sew two leaves to edge of each flower centre, tucking them behind outer round of popcorns and tightening them at the back to make sure they will not come loose. Open the purse frame.

Using C or a contrasting yarn, sew purse front to one side of purse frame, taking the yarn needle into the first hole, coming out at the second, going in at the third and so on all the way around the frame.

Join back of purse to front around the bottom edges with a double crochet seam by working 1 dc through inside loops of both halves all around the bottom, as close as you can go to the purse frame. Make sure that the flowers are RS outwards.

Sew top of purse back to other side of purse frame as before.

EDGING (OPTIONAL)

A decorative edging can be added to either purse if desired. The edging pattern is worked over a multiple of 2 sts. Join B or chosen yarn colour to RS of purse, just below purse frame, and work into double crochet seam as follows:

Row 1: Ch 1, 1 dc in each dc around to opposite side of purse frame, turn. Count number of dc to ensure you have a multiple of 2. If necessary, slip stitches can be worked at beginning or end of next row to achieve required pattern repeat.

Row 2: Ch 3, 3 tr in same place, sl st in next dc, [4 tr in next dc, sl st in next dc] to end.

For a wider shell, work the edging over a multiple of 4 sts + 1, and skip 1 dc before and after each sl st on row 2 to allow the shells to spread out more.

Fasten off and weave in ends.

CLINIC

HOW DO YOU WORK THE EDGING ON TO THE PURSE?

STEP 1

Inserting the hook under both top loops of the double crochet seam, use the slip stitch method to join the edging yarn just below one end of the purse frame.

STEP 2

Work a double crochet into each stitch of the seam all the way around to just below the other end of the purse frame.

STEP 3

Work the scalloped edging pattern into the row of double crochet by working 4 tr into one stitch to create a scallop. Anchor the end of the scallop in place with a slip stitch into the next double crochet.

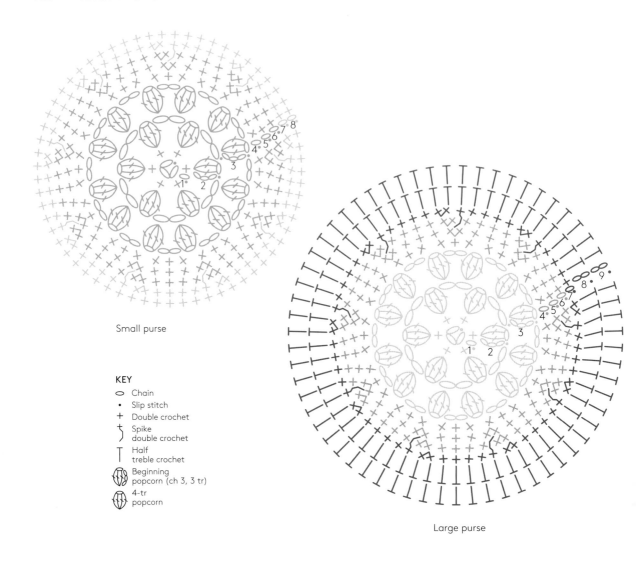

Small purse

Large purse

KEY
○ Chain
• Slip stitch
+ Double crochet
⌇ Spike double crochet
T Half treble crochet
Ⓟ Beginning popcorn (ch 3, 3 tr)
Ⓟ 4-tr popcorn

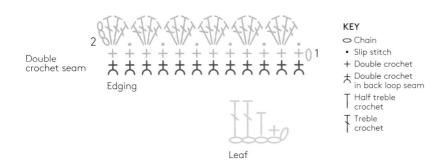

Double crochet seam

Edging

Leaf

KEY
○ Chain
• Slip stitch
+ Double crochet
⋏ Double crochet in back loop seam
T Half treble crochet
T Treble crochet

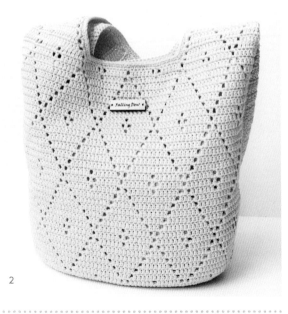

Be inspired

1. KEFALONIA WRAP TOP, ROWAN
This pretty, short-sleeved cardigan with tie-front feature has been created in a cotton yarn to give definition to the simple shell stitches. The solid-colour welt and subtle detailing create a wearable and beautiful item.

2. SHOULDER BAG, RASA GRIGAITE
A simple repeat of treble crochet and chain spaces to create an eyelet pattern has been used to make a practical shoulder bag.

3. MOTHER'S DAY FLOWER BROOCHES, AMY ASTLE
These pretty brooches demonstrate how a simple motif can be transformed into a wearable accessory. Textured stitches, such as puffs and popcorns, are combined with a shell pattern of outer petals to create the three-dimensional texture of the flowers.

4. YELLOW SHAWL, MAAIKE VAN KOERT
The traditional crochet shawl has been updated with luxury yarn. Fan stitches and a lace edging are combined to great effect in this shawl, and the use of a strong colour allows the stitch pattern to stand out and become the main feature of the piece.

5. PINCUSHION,
MAAIKE VAN KOERT
Little popcorn squares have been sewn together and edged in double crochet to make a pretty and useful pincushion. Small motifs are an ideal way to use up leftover yarn from other projects.

6. PUFFY BAND MITTS,
LEONIE MORGAN
The textured band on these mittens has been created using puff stitches. The mittens are worked in the round using a tubular crochet technique, and the shaped thumb is made by increasing stitches.

7. CARMEN TOP, ROWAN
This long-line tee uses a variety of techniques to challenge the crocheter. The result is a stunning and wearable garment. The different shell patterns and taller stitches, such as double trebles, are combined to create a light and airy top.

CHAPTER 4
Finishing Touches

Even the simplest crochet project can be enhanced by careful finishing and small embellishments. From making the perfect buttonhole to adding a handmade edging to a shop-bought item, this chapter will guide you through a range of techniques to give your crochet a professional finish. You will also find tips for embellishing plain projects with beads and decorative trims.

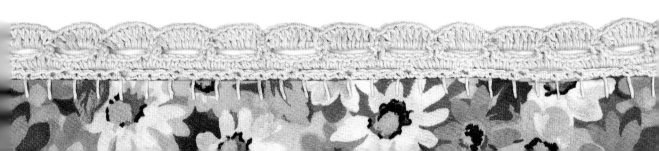

Buttonholes and button loops

The simplest type of buttonhole is a small loop of chain stitches. These can look very attractive on a lightweight garment, but for something more substantial a buttonhole band is needed. These are generally worked in double crochet for stability and strength. Always make the buttonholes before placing the buttons – it is much easier to match buttons up to the buttonhole than the other way around. It is most important that the buttons are evenly spaced.

Horizontal (above) and vertical (far left) buttonholes

VERTICAL BUTTONHOLES

This band can be worked directly on to the edge of a garment. It is helpful to practise making the buttonhole band on your test swatch. You can then take this with you to choose buttons, knowing that the ones you buy will fit properly. The buttonhole is made by working a series of chains over skipped stitches. On the next row, you work into each chain; this leaves a gap in the fabric. The pattern will tell you how big to make the buttonholes and where to place them.

Two rows of double crochet

STEP 1
Practise this technique by working a small band on to a swatch of double crochet. Join the yarn for the buttonhole band to the fabric and work two rows in double crochet.

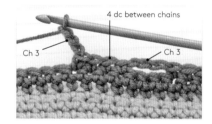

4 dc between chains

Ch 3   Ch 3

STEP 2
On the next row, work at least four double crochet and then start making the buttonholes. Here, each buttonhole is formed by working three chains over three skipped stitches, with four double crochet between each group of chains.

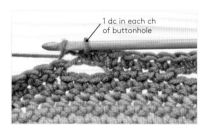

1 dc in each ch of buttonhole

STEP 3
Continue to the end of the row, ending with at least four double crochet. On the next row, make one double crochet in each stitch and one double crochet in each chain to reinforce the buttonholes.

Final row of dc

STEP 4
A final row of double crochet completes the buttonhole band. You can now check the size by slipping a button into the buttonhole.

Button loops

HORIZONTAL BUTTONHOLES

This band is worked as a separate piece and must then be sewn to the crochet fabric. The width of the buttonhole band and the number of rows between each buttonhole depend on how sturdy the band needs to be and the size of the buttons. This example is made with a foundation chain of ten chains (this includes the first turning chain). As you are working in double crochet, remember to make one turning chain at the beginning of each susequent row (this does not count as a stitch).

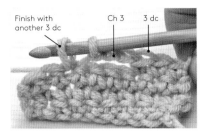

STEP 1
Start by working three rows in double crochet. On the next row, make the first buttonhole using the same technique of chains over skipped stitches as for vertical buttonholes. Here, the row is worked as follows: 3 dc, ch 3, skip 3 sts, 3 dc, turn.

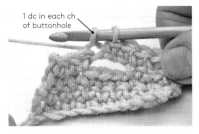

STEP 2
On the following row, make one double crochet in each stitch and one double crochet in each chain to reinforce the buttonholes. Continue in double crochet, making a buttonhole row on every fourth row or as directed in the pattern. See page 43 for advice on sewing the band in place.

BUTTON LOOPS

A row of chain loops made on to the edge of the crochet fabric is the simplest way to make a buttonhole. Because they can be worked directly on to the edge of a garment, there is no need for a button band on the opposite side – buttons can be sewn directly on to the edge of the garment. A stronger and more decorative finish can be achieved by working a second row of double crochet into the chain loops. Usually more chains are made than stitches skipped, to suit the size of button being used.

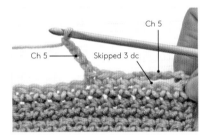

STEP 1
Using the button loop yarn, work one row in double crochet along the edge of the fabric. Work the next row in double crochet up to the position of the first button loop. Make a small loop of chains for the button loop (here, ch 5), skip the required number of stitches (here, skip 3 dc), then continue in double crochet, making more button loops as required.

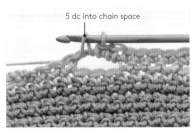

STEP 2
On the following row, work in double crochet up to the first chain loop, then make one double crochet into the chain space for each chain made (in this case, 5 dc). Continue in this way to the end of the row.

ATTACHING A BUTTON

Before you sew on the buttons, always mark where they will be placed first. It is usually best to use a thread in a similar colour to the garment, but you can match the button colour if you prefer. Begin by making a few stitches into the fabric to secure the thread.

SHANKED BUTTON
Sew each button on to the right side of the fabric in the required positions. The shank allows a small space for the bulk of the crochet fabric so that the button band will sit neatly.

FLAT BUTTON
Flat buttons must not be sewn too tightly to the fabric. Traditionally, a matchstick or cocktail stick is placed on top of the button while it is sewn on to the fabric. Once removed, this allows the button room to accommodate the button band.

Crochet cords

Learning to make crochet cords is a valuable and easy skill to master. They can be used instead of ribbons, ties or straps, and wider cords make excellent handles for bags. A spiral cord makes a fun tassel for a scarf. If you require a cord to be a specific length, make a small sample first, count the number of chains made and the length of the finished cord. You can then calculate exactly how many chains you need to make for your crochet cord.

Round cord   Double slip stitch cord   Single slip stitch cord

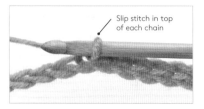

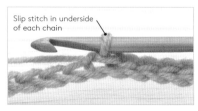

SINGLE SLIP STITCH CORD

Begin with a length of chain. Make a slip stitch into the second chain from the hook and then in each chain to the end. Fasten off and weave in the ends.

DOUBLE SLIP STITCH CORD

For a stronger and more substantial cord, turn the single slip stitch cord and work a second row of slip stitches into the underside of the chain. You may need to use a slightly smaller hook for this.

ROUND CORD

A round cord can be made in the same way as a double crochet spiral cylinder (see page 70). Make five chains, join with a slip stitch and work one double crochet into each chain. Continue to work in a spiral, making one double crochet in each stitch until the cord is the desired length.

DOUBLE CROCHET CORD

Work as for a double slip stitch cord, but use double crochet instead of slip stitch. Using a contrast colour, add a row of slip stitches down the centre using the surface crochet technique (see page 126).

Double crochet cord   Spiral cord

SPIRAL CORD

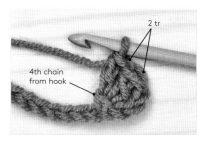

STEP 1
Start with a chain of any length and work 2 tr into the fourth chain from the hook.

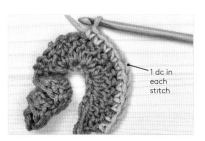

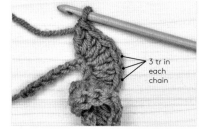

STEP 2
Work 3 tr into each chain to the end. As you work along the chain, you will see the work begin to spiral.

STEP 3
To add a striped edge, join in a contrasting colour yarn and work 1 dc into the top of each treble. Spiral cords can be worked in other crochet stitches using the same basic technique.

Edgings

An edging can be used to neaten the edge on a piece of crochet or simply to add a contrasting colour or texture to a finished piece. If you are crocheting an edging on an item that has a seam, start the edging away from the seam to make the join less noticeable. It is recommended that you use the same yarn composition for the edging as for the main project. This will prevent the crochet from distorting when it is washed.

Reverse

Front

CRAB STITCH EDGING

This is worked from left to right and is made directly on to the right side of the fabric. Sometimes called a corded edge, it gives a firm, stable edging to the crochet. The technique can feel awkward at first because the hook is moving in a different way from usual, but do keep practising as this stitch is such a useful technique that you will be glad you persevered.

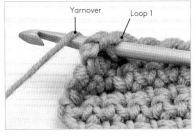

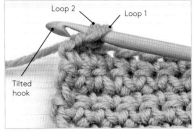

STEP 1
A contrast colour is used for clarity here, but it can also be used for decorative effect. At the end of the row, do not turn. Working from left to right, insert the hook into the next stitch on the right. Wrap the yarn over the hook.

STEP 2
Draw the yarn through to the front of the work, tilting the hook slightly so that the loops do not slip off (you will have two loops on the hook).

STEP 3
Bring the hook back to its normal position and wrap the yarn over the hook again. Draw it through both loops to complete the first crab stitch. Continue to the end of the row, working left to right and making one crab stitch into each stitch along the row.

CLINIC

HOW DO I CROCHET AN EDGING AROUND A CORNER?

You need to work extra stitches at the corner, otherwise the crochet fabric will pucker and distort. The taller the stitch you are using, the more stitches you will need to work into the corner. Your pattern will tell you how many stitches to make, but in general three double crochet or five trebles will suffice. Practise the edging pattern first on your tension swatch.

PICOT EDGING

This is a very elegant edging and is suitable for almost any project. Small chains are anchored on each side with a slip stitch or double crochet. You can vary the number of chains and anchoring stitches to suit the project.

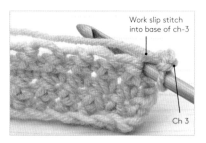

STEP 1
Make three chains (or number required) and then slip stitch into the stitch at the base of the chains. This forms the first picot. Make one double crochet in the next stitch.

STEP 2
Make the next picot by working one double crochet into the next stitch, then make three chains followed by a slip stitch into the same stitch.

STEP 3
Continue working picots along the edge, separated by one double crochet stitch.

SHELL EDGING

A shell edge is a very dainty and pretty trim, often used on doilies and homewares. It is easiest to work a shell edging on to straight edges or round items, because corners can be tricky to negotiate. The simple shell pattern shown here is worked over a multiple of 6 sts + 1. You will need to count your stitches.

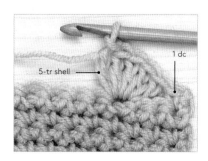

STEP 1
If you are working in a contrasting colour, begin by making a row of double crochet before working the shell edging (this gives a much crisper colour transition that is more professional and pleasing to the eye). Turn the work and make one turning chain. Make one double crochet in the first stitch, skip the next two stitches, then make five trebles in the next stitch (one shell made).

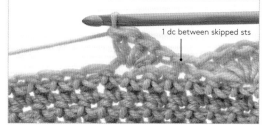

STEP 2
Skip the next two stitches and make one double crochet in the next stitch. This anchors the end of the first shell.

STEP 3
Continue to work in pattern to the end of the row as follows: *skip 2 dc, 5 tr in next dc, skip 2 dc, 1 dc in next dc; repeat from * to end.

CLINIC

I DON'T HAVE ENOUGH STITCHES TO WORK A COMPLETE REPEAT OF THE EDGING AT THE END OF MY ROW. WHAT SHOULD I DO?

You can easily remedy this. Count the stitches and divide them by the multiple given for the pattern (remember to allow for any turning chains), then simply work half the remainder in slip stitch at each end of the edging row. For example, if you have four extra stitches, work two slip stitches at each end of the row.

7 QUICK EDGING TRICKS

1 Adding an edging is a useful way of adding length to a child's garment when it is outgrown but still in good condition.

2 Adding an edging in a contrasting or harmonious colour is a quick way to liven up plain crochet. Or, give last season's T-shirts a new lease of life with a pretty shell trim around the hemline.

3 A simple edging in the same colour as the main crochet fabric is a great way to cover up an uneven edge. Missed a turning chain? Don't worry; a simple edging can disguise all manner of mistakes.

4 A shell edging makes a pretty buttonhole, especially for baby clothes. Work the shell edging described on the left, but work 2 tr, ch 1, 2 tr in place of 5 tr and use the ch-1 space as a buttonhole.

5 Add a unique twist to a shop-bought jumper by crocheting an edging to the hem and cuffs.

6 Almost every crochet blanket benefits from a crochet trim to neaten edges. Even a simple double crochet border can really make a difference and is an easy way to disguise any messy colour changes.

7 Add a personal touch to shop-bought table linens with a crochet border. Use a colour that matches your decor, or use complementary colours to make a bridal or housewarming gift (if your sewing skills are up to the job, try embroidering the recipients' initials or the date of their wedding in one corner).

ADDING A CROCHET EDGING TO FABRIC

A crochet edge is a traditional way to brighten up household items, such as table linens and pillowcases. You can also use the technique to refresh a favourite garment, such as the collar and cuffs or the hem of a T-shirt. You can either make the trim first and then sew it on, or sew blanket stitches to the edge of the fabric and then use them as a foundation for working the first row of crochet. When sewing the foundation row of blanket stitch, try not to work the stitches too tightly or the crochet rows will pucker.

BLANKET STITCH

Use a sewing thread that matches the yarn for the crochet trim. Embroidery thread is ideal because the wide range of colours available makes it easy to match it to the yarn.

Leave loop at front

STEP 1
Secure the thread to the back of the fabric at the right-hand edge. Bring the needle through to the front, about 6mm (¼in) in from the edge. Then take the needle through to the back again, slightly to the left.

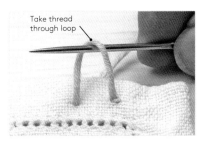

Take thread through loop

STEP 2
Leave a loop of thread at the front, then bring the needle up above the fabric from behind and take it through the loop to complete the first blanket stitch.

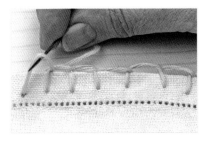

STEP 3
Continue in this way until you reach the end of the fabric. Try to keep the stitches evenly spaced and equal in length. You can mark the distance between each stitch using an air-soluble fabric pencil before you begin.

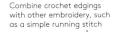
Combine crochet edgings with other embroidery, such as a simple running stitch

Joining motifs

You can join motifs together using any of the seaming techniques in chapter 1 (see pages 43–45). Alternatively, motifs can be 'joined as you go' by crocheting them together on the final round. There are several methods and whole books devoted to joining techniques for crochet motifs, so it is essential to read the pattern through first and, if possible, follow the chart because it often makes it clearer to see where the joins are made.

JOINING AS YOU GO

This simple method is sometimes called a flat join because the resulting join is a smooth and unobtrusive flat seam (for an alternative join-as-you-go method using slip stitches, see page 134). This example shows the granny squares from page 65 being joined together. Complete the first motif and then work the second motif as far as the final round.

STEP 1
Join the yarn for the final round into any corner chain space of the second motif. Work the first side of the square as usual as far as the second corner – in this example, (3 tr, ch 3, 3 tr) in first corner ch sp, ch 1, [3 tr in next ch sp, ch 1] twice.

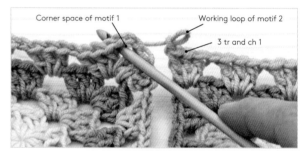

STEP 2
Work the second corner up to the halfway point – here, 3 tr, ch 1. Remove the hook from the working loop, then insert the hook from front to back into any corner chain space on the first motif.

STEP 3
Put the working loop back on the hook and draw the loop through the corner chain space of the first motif to the front.

STEP 4
Complete the corner by working ch 1, 3 tr. The two squares are now joined at the corner. Note that pulling the working loop through the adjoining motif (the joining loop) replaces the middle chain usually worked at the corner.

Pull working loop through each chain space along side of motif 1

STEP 5
Continue to work the final round of the second motif, joining the squares at each chain space along the side edge in the same way as at the corner by taking the working loop off the hook, inserting the hook into the next chain space along the side of the first motif and drawing the loop through to the front. Then make the usual one chain and three trebles in the next chain space along the side of the second motif.

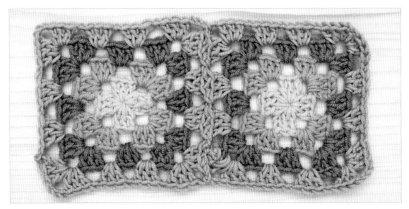

STEP 6
When you reach the next corner, join the two squares as before and then complete the final round of the second motif. The two squares are now joined together along one side.

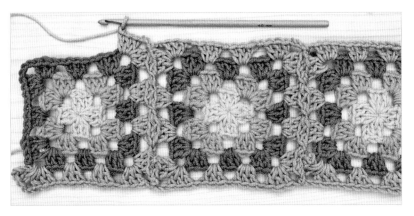

STEP 7
To make a strip of motifs, simply carry on joining further motifs in the same way, joining them at two corners and along one side edge.

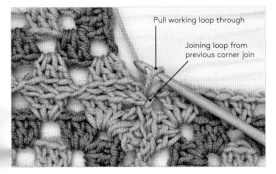

Pull working loop through

Joining loop from previous corner join

STEP 8
You can use the same technique to join the motifs along more than one side. Always remember to join the motifs in every chain space along each side and to make the usual chain to travel between sets of three trebles. When you reach a corner where more than two motifs adjoin, insert the hook into the previous joining loop – that is, into the working loop that was pulled through the corner space during the earlier join – rather than into a corner space to make a neater transition.

Embellishments

There are numerous ways of embellishing your crochet. Surface crochet is worked directly on to the right side of the finished crochet fabric using slip stitches. It can be used to add a pop of colour or to introduce texture to a plain project. Other effective embellishments include motifs such as flowers and beads or sequins. Beads can be sewn on to the finished crochet fabric but the most secure way to attach them is to work them in with the crochet stitches.

SURFACE CROCHET

This is sometimes called the tambour method, after a technique used in embroidery. The yarn is held at the back of the work, while the design is made on to the right side of the fabric using a crochet hook and a series of slip stitches. This example shows surface crochet worked on to a double crochet swatch, but you can work surface crochet on to any crochet stitch. Beautiful effects can be achieved by working on to mesh fabric (see page 97).

STEP 1
Make a slip knot in the yarn and place it at the back of the work. Insert the hook through the fabric from front to back, pick up the slip knot and draw it through to the front of the fabric.

STEP 2
Insert the hook into the fabric from front to back between the next pair of stitches, wrap the yarn over the hook and draw a loop through to the front. Draw up a slightly looser loop than for normal crochet to avoid puckering the fabric.

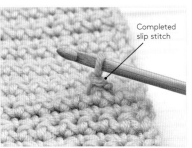

STEP 3
Pull the second loop through the first to complete the slip stitch.

STEP 4
Repeat as many times as required. You can work in straight lines, following the stitches and rows on the crochet fabric, or make patterns by inserting the hook into a different place each time.

Layered flower

Worked in two colours, A and B.

Foundation ring: Using A, ch 6 and join with sl st to form a ring.

Round 1: Ch 5 (counts as 1 tr, ch 2), [1 tr into ring, ch 2] 7 times, join with sl st to 3rd ch of beg ch-5. (8 tr, 8 ch sp)

Round 2: Sl st into next ch sp, (1 dc, 3 tr, 1 dc) in same ch sp, [1 dc, 3 tr, 1 dc in next ch sp] 7 times, join with sl st to first dc.
Fasten off A. Turn flower over and, working into the wrong side, join B to the post of any tr.

Round 3: Ch 6 (counts as 1 tr, ch 3), [1 FPtr around next tr, ch 3] 7 times, join with sl st to 3rd ch of beg ch-6.
Turn flower over and work next round with right side facing.

Round 4: Ch 1, (1 dc, 5 tr, 1 dc) in each ch-3 sp around, join with sl st to first dc.
Fasten off and weave in ends.

KEY
- ⌒ Chain
- • Slip stitch
- + Double crochet
- ⊤ Half treble crochet
- ⊤ Treble crochet
- ⌡ Front post treble crochet
- ↗ Direction of work

SEW-ON FLOWER MOTIF

Use crochet flowers to add the finishing touch to accessories, such as hats and bags, or stitch one to a brooch pin to wear on any garment. This flower uses a simple technique to create a second layer of petals behind the first layer for a three-dimensional motif. After making the first round of petals, the flower is turned over and a round of chains and trebles form the base for a second row of petals. You can add extra layers of petals using the same principle.

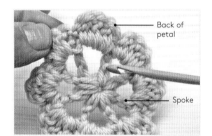

Back of petal

Spoke

STEP 1
Follow the layered flower pattern to the end of round 2 (see above). You will have eight clearly spaced trebles and eight petals. Turn the flower over. The posts of the trebles form spokes and it is around these that you will work the base for the next layer of petals.

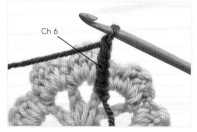

Ch 6

STEP 2
Using a slip stitch, join the yarn for the second layer of petals around the post of any treble of round 1. Make six chains.

Work tr around spoke

STEP 3
Work a treble around the post of the next treble of round 1, inserting the hook around the post from the side facing you.

Chain spaces for working petals

STEP 4
Continue working lengths of chain joined to the posts of round 1 with a treble crochet. Join the round by making a slip stitch into the third chain of the beginning ch-6.

Work from right side

STEP 5
Make sure that you turn the flower over so the right side is facing you before beginning the next round. Work round 4 to create the petals.

BEADED CROCHET

Beads can easily be applied to your crochet project as you work and are very effective on a piece of plain double crochet. The simplest way to add beads is to string them on to the yarn before you begin and then add them to the fabric as you crochet.

STRINGING THE BEADS

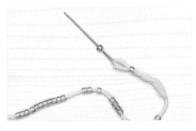

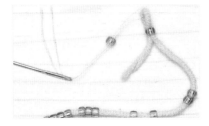

METHOD 1

For lighter weight yarns, you may be able to thread the yarn through a tapestry needle and simply pass the beads down the needle and on to the yarn. You can also buy special beading needles that have a big eye that is large enough accommodate yarn.

METHOD 2

For bulkier yarns, thread the needle with some sewing thread and tie the ends in a knot. Pass the yarn through the loop in the sewing thread. You can now thread the beads on to the needle and push them down the needle, along the thread and on to the yarn.

3   TIPS FOR SUCCESSFUL BEADING

1 Always check that the beads are large enough to slip on to the yarn. If you are working from a pattern, the designer will tell you what size beads to use, such as size 6 beads with DK yarn.

2 Begin by winding the yarn to check for any knots; the beads will not be able to pass over them and it can be very frustrating to encounter knots when you have already begun your project.

3 Always thread more beads than you think you need as it is easy to lose count. It is far better to have beads left over than to run out before completing the project.

BEADED DOUBLE CROCHET

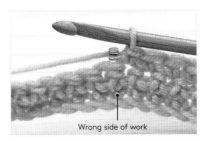

Wrong side of work

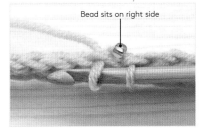

Bead sits on right side

STEP 1

Beads are added on wrong side rows. Work to the position of the first bead, then slide the bead along the yarn until it sits as close to the hook as possible.

STEP 2

Insert the hook into the next stitch, wrap the yarn over the hook and draw a loop through. As you do so, make sure the bead stays in place; it will be secured on the right side of the work as you complete the stitch. Continue adding beads as required.

STEP 3

Work a row of double crochet without beads. Remember that beads are placed on wrong side rows and so are worked every other row, unless you want to create a reversible fabric.

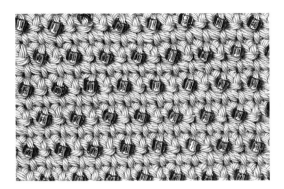

Alternating beads

SPECIAL STITCH

Bdc: Work a beaded double crochet by inserting hook into next stitch, yo, pull loop through, slide bead as close as possible to hook, yo, pull through both loops on hook.

Foundation chain: Make a multiple of 3 ch + 1.
Ch 1 at beginning of rows counts as 1 dc throughout.
Row 1: 1 dc in second ch from hook, 1 dc in each ch to end, turn.
Row 2: Ch 1, 1 dc in each dc to end, turn.
Row 3: Ch 1, skip first dc, 1 dc in each dc to end, turn.
Row 4: Ch 1, skip first dc, 1 dc in each of next 2 dc, *1 Bdc in next dc, 1 dc in next dc; rep from * to last st, 1 dc in last dc, turn.
Row 5: As row 3.
Row 6: Ch 1, skip first dc, 1 dc in each of next 3 dc, *1 Bdc in next dc, 1 dc in next dc; rep from * to last 2 sts, 1 dc in each of last 2 dc, turn.
Repeat rows 3–6 for pattern, ending with three rows of double crochet.

All-over sequins

Follow the alternating beads pattern (see left), but use sequins instead of beads. Take care to choose the right size of sequin. If the sequin is too small for the weight of the yarn, it will not lie flat, so it is a good idea to test this before starting on a project. If using cup-shaped sequins rather than the flat ones (shown here), make sure to string them on to the yarn so that the convex side (the bottom of the cup) of each sequin faces towards the ball of yarn. When crocheted, the cup will then face away from the crochet fabric. Knitting sequins have larger holes than ordinary ones, and they are often sold threaded on to a loop of strong thread. To use the sequins, cut the loop, knot one end of the thread on to the yarn, and carefully slide the sequins over the knot and on to the yarn.

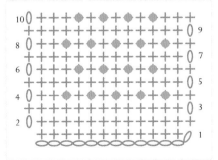

CLINIC

I HAVEN'T STRUNG ENOUGH BEADS ON TO MY YARN. IS THERE A WAY TO ADD A FEW MORE WITHOUT HAVING TO CUT AND REJOIN THE YARN?

There are other techniques for adding beads to your crochet, such as using a very fine crochet hook to place each bead as you work. For example, put the bead on to the fine hook, transfer the working loop to this hook, slide the bead down on to the yarn and then transfer the loop back on to the original hook to work the crochet stitch. This is more difficult, but it means that you do not need to thread the beads on to the yarn first. If you are using lots of different-coloured beads or only placing beads in one part of your crochet, this can be a helpful technique.

KEY

⊃ Chain
+ Double crochet
◆ Beaded double crochet

Quick start project:

Pillowcase edgings

Use these pretty shell and picot edgings to brighten up your bedroom linen. They are applied all around the opening of the pillowcases, so there are no tricky corners to negotiate.

FINISHED SIZE
To fit any size of pillowcase

TENSION
Scalloped shells: 3½ repeats = 10cm (4in) long
Picot crowns: 3½ repeats = 10cm (4in) long
Long scallops: 3½ repeats = 10cm (4in) long

YOU WILL NEED
- 1 ball of 4ply-weight cotton yarn per pillowcase; Tracey used DMC Natura Just Cotton, 100% cotton with approx. 155m (170yd) per 50g ball, in Rose Layette 06, Blue Layette 05 and Ivory 02, and DMC Petra size 3 crochet thread, 100% cotton with approx. 280m (306yd) per 100g ball, in Red 5321, but any 4ply cotton yarn can be substituted
- 3mm crochet hook
- Yarn needle
- Sharp needle to sew blanket stitch

ABBREVIATIONS AND TECHNIQUES
beg = beginning
ch = chain (page 18)
dc = double crochet (page 23)
rep = repeat
sp = space
st(s) = stitch(es)
tr = treble crochet (page 25)
Decreasing (pages 38–39)
Edgings (page 121–123)

PATTERN NOTES
- A stitch multiple is given for each edging so that you can adjust as necessary to suit the size of item that you are edging. The edgings shown here are crocheted directly on to the pillowcases, but if you prefer they can be worked separately and then sewn on.
- The charts include a foundation chain shaded in grey. You only need to make this chain if you have decided to work the edgings separately. Omit the chain if you are attaching the edgings using blanket stitch. If using blanket stitch, two stitches of the pattern are worked into each blanket stitch.
- Ch 1 at the beginning of rows does not count as a stitch.

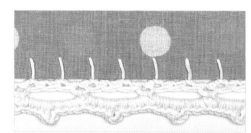
Picot crowns edging

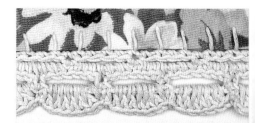
Long scallops edging

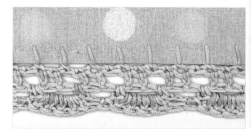
Scalloped shells edging

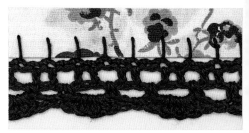
Scalloped shells edging

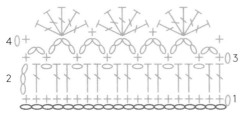

KEY
◯ Chain
+ Double crochet
T Treble
 crochet

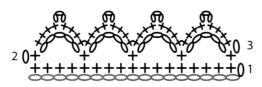

KEY
◯ Chain
+ Double crochet

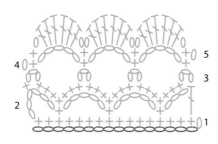

KEY
◯ Chain
+ Double crochet
T Treble
 crochet

BLANKET STITCH FOUNDATION
Using the same yarn colour that you will use for the crochet edging, sew blanket stitch around the edge of each pillowcase.
To work the crochet edging, join the yarn to any blanket stitch closest to one of the side seams and follow your chosen edging pattern below.

SCALLOPED SHELLS
Pattern is worked over a multiple of 6 sts + 2.
In example shown, there are 158 dc worked into 79 blanket stitches around the edge.
Row 1: Ch 1, 2 dc in each blanket st to end, turn.
Row 2: Ch 3 (counts as 1 tr), skip first dc, 1 tr in next dc, *ch 1, skip next dc, 1 tr in each of next 2 dc; rep from * to end, turn.
Row 3: Ch 1, 1 dc in first tr, ch 2, 1 dc in next ch-1 sp, *ch 4, 1 dc in next ch-1 sp; rep from * to last 2 sts, ch 2, 1 tr in top of beg ch-3, turn.
Row 4: Ch 1, 1 dc in first dc, skip ch-2 sp, *5 tr in next ch-4 sp, 1 dc in next ch-4 sp; rep from * to last ch-2 sp, skip last ch-2 sp, 1 dc in last dc.
Fasten off, leaving a long tail. Sew side seam using tail.

PICOT CROWNS
Pattern is worked over a multiple of 4 sts + 2.
In example shown, there are 158 dc worked into 79 blanket stitches around the edge.
Row 1: Ch 1, 2 dc in each blanket st to end, turn.
Row 2: Ch 1, 1 dc in first dc, *ch 5, skip next 3 dc, 1 dc in next dc; rep from * to end, turn.
Row 3: Ch 1, *[4 dc, ch 3 (picot made), 4 dc] in next ch-5 sp; rep from * to end.
Fasten off, leaving a long tail. Sew side seam using tail.

LONG SCALLOPS
Pattern is worked over a multiple of 5 sts + 1.
In example shown, there are 160 dc worked into 80 blanket stitches around the edge.
Row 1: Ch 1, 2 dc in each blanket st to end, turn.
Row 2: Ch 6, skip first 2 dc, 1 dc in next dc, *ch 5, skip next 4 dc, 1 dc in next dc; rep from * to last 3 dc, ch 3, skip next 2 dc, 1 tr in last dc, turn.
Row 3: Ch 3 (counts as first picot), 3 dc in first ch-3 sp, 1 dc in next dc (between chain loops), *(3 dc, ch 3 [picot made], 3 dc) in next ch-5 sp, 1 dc in next dc; rep from * ending (3 dc, ch 3, 1 dc) in last ch-6 sp, turn.
Row 4: Ch 1, 1 dc in first ch-3 picot, *ch 5, 1 dc in next ch-3 picot; rep from * to end, turn.
Row 5: Ch 1, 1 dc in first dc, *ch 1, 6 tr in next ch-5 sp, ch 1, 1 dc in next dc; rep from * to end.
Fasten off, leaving a long tail. Sew side seam using tail.

Guest Designer Leonie Morgan

I'm a crochet addict with a large yarn stash and more crochet blankets than I'll ever need! I love designing with colour. I prefer Aran or DK yarn and a nice big hook, and just love motifs and blocks. Whatever I'm designing, the colour choice is the exciting bit. I enjoy the process of designing, from initial fumblings with scrap yarn to picking colours and writing patterns. My hands hate to be idle, so I always have a hook and yarn in my bag ready to whip up some crochet loveliness. You can see more of my work at www.leoniemorgan.com.

Flower blanket

This pattern is designed to use up scraps of yarn, applying the join-as-you-go method to keep adding motifs to the blanket until you reach the size you want. Each flower is worked in random colours from a 10-colour yarn palette. Including one or two neutrals in the palette will help to make the bright colours really pop.

FINISHED SIZE
89 x 112cm (35 x 44in)

TENSION
Each flower motif measures 7.5 x 7.5cm (3 x 3in)

YOU WILL NEED
- 2 x 50g balls of DK-weight wool yarn in each of 10 colours; Leonie used DMC Woolly, 100% merino wool with approx. 125m (136yd) per ball, in 03, 054, 055, 063, 073, 084, 094, 102, 111 and 112, but any DK yarn can be substituted
- 4.5mm crochet hook
- Yarn needle

ABBREVIATIONS AND TECHNIQUES
ch = chain (page 18)
dc = double crochet (page 23)
rep = repeat
sl st = slip stitch (page 22)
sp = space
st(s) = stitch(es)
tr = treble crochet (page 25)
Magic ring (pages 56–57)
Joining motifs (page 124)
Surface crochet (page 126)

PATTERN NOTES
- A magic ring is used to start the motif because it creates a closed, solid centre to mimic the eye of a real flower.
- A ch-3 space is worked at each petal tip, providing shape to the petals and a convenient place to join the motifs with slip stitches.
- Where four flowers join together, three of the flowers are joined to the remaining flower. You can vary this joining arrangement if you wish, but try to be consistent for neatness.
- Surface crochet is used to frame the eye of the flower. A contrasting colour will give the best impact.

FLOWER 1

Foundation ring: Using first colour, make a magic ring.
Round 1: Ch 1, 8 dc into ring, join with sl st to first dc.
(8 dc)
Change to second colour.
Round 2: *Ch 3, 1 tr in same place, (1 tr, ch 3, sl st) in
next dc, sl st in next dc; rep from * 3 times more ending
sl st into base of beg ch-3. (8 ch-3, 8 tr)
Round 3: *Ch 3, 3 tr in next tr, ch 3 (petal tip made),
3 tr in next tr, ch 3, sl st into each of next 2 sl st; rep
from * 3 times more. (24 tr)
Fasten off.
Surface crochet: With a contrasting colour, sl st into
each dc on round 1.

ALL REMAINING FLOWERS

Follow flower 1 instructions as far as the end of round 2.
Round 3 (joining round): *Ch 3, 3 tr in next tr; when
joining to another flower work (ch 1, sl st into ch-3 petal
tip of adjoining flower, ch 1); if not joining to another
flower work ch 3; then work 3 tr in next tr, sl st into each
of next 2 sl st; rep from * 3 times more.
Add surface crochet as for flower 1.
To make the blanket, join flowers in 20 rows of 14 flowers.

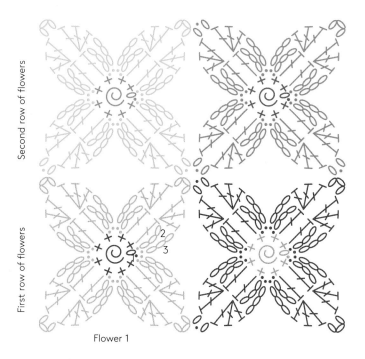

First row of flowers

Second row of flowers

Flower 1

KEY

- ⟲ Magic ring
- ⌒ Chain
- • Slip stitch
- + Double crochet
- T Treble crochet

CLINIC ⊕ : HOW DO YOU
JOIN MOTIFS USING
THE JOIN-AS-YOU-
GO SLIP STITCH
METHOD?

STEP 1
Work round 3 of the flower as far as
the petal tip. Instead of working the
usual ch 3, work ch 1 and then insert
the hook into the ch-3 space at the
tip of the adjoining flower petal.
Work a slip stitch in this space to
join the flowers, then finish with ch 1.

STEP 2
Continue working the final round of
the flower, joining to the petal tips of
adjacent flowers as necessary with a
slip stitch.

Be inspired

1. CROCHET-EMBELLISHED COAT, SIDSEL J. HØIVIK

Tiny motifs in many different colours have been stitched on to this knitted coat. Combining the crafts of knitting and crochet is not new, but today's designers are combining the two crafts in imaginative ways, such as using crochet embellishments to add vibrant colour to a plain knitted garment.

2. MAISY BARRETTE, KATE GREEN

This simple hair accessory demonstrates how versatile crochet motifs can be. Using simple stitches, bright colours and surface crochet details, you can find a practical use for almost any small crochet motif. A barrette bar or brooch pin sewn to the reverse allows the motif to be worn in a variety of ways.

3. GREY BLANKET, MAAIKE VAN KOERT

Square motifs are combined with a puff stitch edging for a modern interpretation of the granny square blanket. Using a single colour makes the texture the star of the show. The motifs are joined using double crochet seam and the edging is worked around the completed blanket.

4. FLOWER TIE-BACK,
SANDRA PAUL
A combination of flat and layered
crochet flowers are joined on to a
crochet chain, showing once again
how versatile crochet motifs can be.
A similar effect could be created using
any decorative crochet motifs, made
in colours to suit your own decor.

5. BABY PONCHO,
MAAIKE VAN KOERT
Using a limited colour palette and
a textured motif, the designer has
updated the traditional granny square
poncho. Textured stitches such as
bobbles have been used to add interest,
and the motifs have been joined using
the join-as-you-go method on the final
round. A ribbon tie at the neck is used
to fasten the poncho.

6. FLORAL SHAWL, ROWAN
Layered flowers have been joined
together to create a beautiful and
delicate shawl. This vintage-style piece
demonstrates how traditional crochet
techniques have their place in modern
fashion collections. This piece could be
worn on many occasions and would
quickly become a treasured item.

CHAPTER 5
Taking Your Skills Further

Once you have practised the standard crochet stitches, it can be fun to experiment with new techniques such as Tunisian, broomstick and hairpin crochet. These techniques are not difficult, but it helps if you are already comfortable with the basics and are familiar with reading crochet patterns. You will also find some advice at the end of this chapter on finessing your crochet – hints and tips for achieving a more professional finish, and variations on basic techniques that are fun to learn and useful to know.

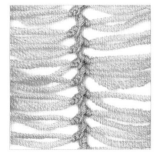

Tunisian crochet

Also known as Afghan crochet, this technique has a long history and is growing in popularity. It is now becoming easier to find patterns for garments and accessories that use this technique. Tunisian crochet produces a firm fabric, ideal for blankets and accessories.

UNDERSTANDING THE BASICS

There are a few tools and terms not used in traditional crochet; here they are explained to help you get started.

TUNISIAN HOOKS

You will need a special Tunisian hook. There are two common types. The first is like a standard hook, but with a much longer shaft and a fixed stopper at the end to prevent stitches from sliding off. The second type has a flexible cord attached to a standard hook. Sometimes these cords are interchangeable so that the cord length can be adjusted to suit your project or attached to different-sized hooks. To achieve the required drape for a garment, you may need to use a larger hook than usually specified for the weight of yarn.

HOW IT WORKS

Each row of Tunisian crochet is made up of two passes. The forward pass is the process of making stitches and adding loops to the hook. The return pass works the loops off the hook again. The same side of the crochet is always facing you for both passes, and there is no need to work a turning chain.

TUNISIAN CHARTS

Just like traditional crochet, a Tunisian pattern may be accompanied by a chart. Only the forward pass is shown on the chart, and it is assumed that the crocheter will know to complete a return pass before beginning the next row.

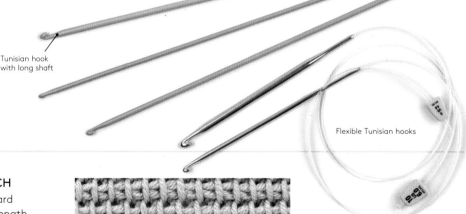

Stopper

Tunisian hook with long shaft

Flexible Tunisian hooks

TUNISIAN SIMPLE STITCH

Begin by making a standard foundation chain of any length. Note that the forward pass is worked from right to left, and the return pass from left to right without turning the work.

Repeat row 2 for pattern

KEY

$\sim$ Tunisian
| simple stitch
← Forward pass
→ Return pass

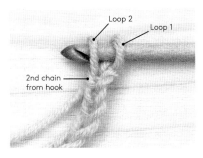

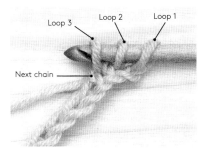

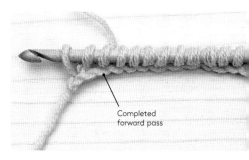

STEP 1
Begin the first forward pass by inserting the hook into the second chain from the hook. Wrap the yarn over and pull a loop through, giving you two loops on the hook. Each loop counts as a stitch.

STEP 2
Insert the hook into the next chain, wrap the yarn over and pull through, giving three loops on the hook.

STEP 3
Repeat until you have made a loop from each foundation chain and have a row of loops on the hook. You should have the same number of loops as foundation chains. Do not turn the work.

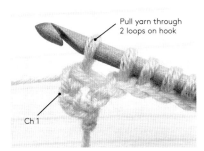

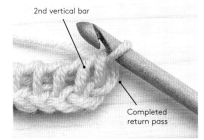

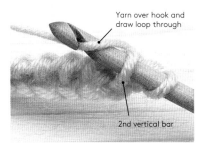

STEP 4
Begin the first return pass by wrapping the yarn over the hook and drawing it through the first loop on the hook to make one chain; this completes the first stitch. Wrap the yarn over again and draw it through the first two loops on the hook; this completes the second stitch.

STEP 5
Continue working along the hook, wrapping the yarn over the hook and pulling it through two loops at a time until you have one loop on the hook. Note the pattern of vertical bars at the front of the work.

STEP 6
To work the next forward pass, skip the first vertical bar and insert the hook from right to left under the second vertical bar (not through to the back of the work). Wrap the yarn over the hook and draw through to make a second loop on the hook.

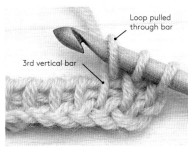

STEP 8
At the end of the row, make a return pass as described in steps 4–5. Continue working a forward pass (steps 6–7) followed by a return pass (steps 4–5) until the work is the required size. Make sure to end with a return pass. Fasten off the crochet in the usual way or as described on page 142.

STEP 7
Insert the hook under the next vertical bar, wrap the yarn over and draw a loop through. You should now have three loops on the hook. Continue to the end of the row.

FINISHING TUNISIAN CROCHET

Sometimes a Tunisian pattern will instruct you to finish with a row of standard treble crochet to neaten and strengthen the last row. Another method of achieving a neater and more professional finish is to work a Tunisian cast off, especially when the edge will be seen on the finished project. Use whichever method you prefer.

Work 1 tr through each vertical bar

THINGS TO REMEMBER ABOUT TUNISIAN CROCHET

1 Each Tunisian row needs both a forward and a return pass, ending with a single loop on the hook at the end of the return pass.

2 Never turn the work at the end of a row. Always make sure to work a return pass to complete each row.

3 The first loop on the hook counts as the first stitch of the row.

TREBLE CROCHET FINISH

After completing the final return pass, make one turning chain. Then insert the hook from right to left under the second vertical bar, wrap the yarn over and pull a loop through (2 loops on hook). Wrap the yarn over again and pull through both loops on the hook to complete the treble crochet stitch. Continue working one treble crochet into each vertical bar across the row. Fasten off in the usual way.

Treble crochet finish on a swatch of Tunisian simple stitch

TUNISIAN CAST OFF

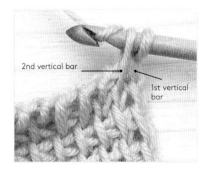

2nd vertical bar

1st vertical bar

Front and back vertical bars of last stitch

STEP 1
After completing the final return pass and with one loop on the hook, insert the hook from right to left under the second vertical bar at the front of the work. Wrap the yarn over the hook and pull through both loops on the hook.

STEP 2
Continue to the last stitch. Instead of inserting the hook under the front vertical bar only, this time insert it under both the front and back vertical bars of the last stitch. Wrap the yarn over the hook and pull through all loops on the hook. Fasten off in the usual way.

STEP 3
The Tunisian cast off has been worked on a swatch of Tunisian simple stitch here, so that you can directly compare the finished result with the treble crochet finish above, but it works particularly well with Tunisian knit stitch (see opposite).

TUNISIAN KNIT STITCH

This variation of Tunisian crochet produces a fabric that closely resembles knitted stocking stitch on the right side. The edges will curl as you make this swatch, but blocking will help to fix this.

Repeat row 2 for pattern

KEY

$\widetilde{\top}$ Tunisian simple stitch

$\widetilde{V}$ Tunisian knit stitch

← Forward pass

→ Return pass

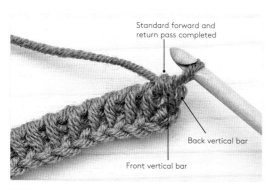

Standard forward and return pass completed

Back vertical bar

Front vertical bar

Horizontal loops on top

Insert hook between front and back vertical bars

STEP 1

Begin by making a standard forward and return pass as for Tunisian simple stitch (see page 141, steps 1–5). Note that each stitch has a vertical loop, composed of a front and back vertical bar.

STEP 2

To begin the next forward pass, skip the first vertical bar and insert the hook between the front and back vertical bars of the second stitch and through to the back of the work, under the two horizontal loops that lie above the stitch. Wrap the yarn over the hook and pull a loop through, giving you two loops on the hook.

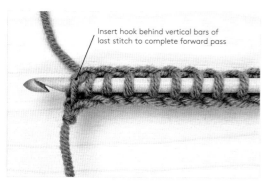

Insert hook behind vertical bars of last stitch to complete forward pass

Standard return pass

STEP 3

Continue to work along the row, inserting the hook between the vertical bars and under the horizontal loops of each stitch. When you reach the end of the row, insert the hook into the last stitch as shown – that is, insert the hook through the fabric behind both the front and back vertical bars instead of between them. Make sure to count your stitches at the end of the row (the last stitch is often missed).

STEP 4

Work a standard return pass in the same way as for Tunisian simple stitch (page 141, steps 4–5). After a few rows, you will see the stitch pattern emerge and notice the similarity to knitted stocking stitch. Fasten off in the usual way or as described on page 142.

Hairpin crochet

Also known as hairpin lace, this is a quick way to produce lacy strips or braids of loose crochet. In Victorian times, it was popular for edgings and trims. Once made, the strips can be joined together with standard crochet stitches. Today, many crochet designers are incorporating hairpin techniques into crochet garments and accessories, introducing the technique to a new audience.

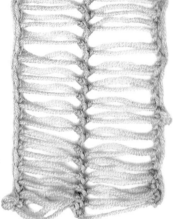

UNDERSTANDING THE BASICS

There are a few tools and terms not used in traditional crochet; here they are explained to help you get started.

HAIRPIN TOOLS

You will need to buy a hairpin lace loom. Sometimes called netting forks, these are widely available and inexpensive. They can be a fixed width or adjustable; the latter allows you to make different widths of crochet. You will also need a standard crochet hook, in a size smaller than usual for the weight of yarn.

HOW IT WORKS

The crochet hook is used to make a series of loops of yarn between the two pins or prongs on the loom until the loom is full of loops. The strip is then removed by taking all the loops off the loom. As you become more proficient, it is possible to remove some loops and continue working to make a longer strip. Once completed, you can either use the braid just as it is, or work a row of double crochet along each looped edge for extra stability. It is easier to follow the technique by trying it for yourself – as with many crochet techniques, once practised, the principle becomes easier to understand.

SIMPLE HAIRPIN BRAID

This example is made using a fixed loom. If you are using an adjustable loom, set the prongs 10cm (4in) apart to make a similar width strip.

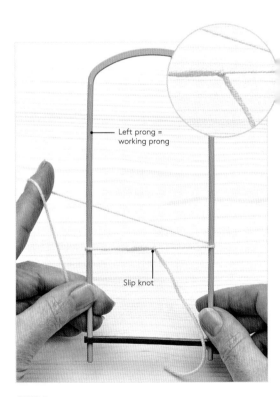

Left prong = working prong

Slip knot

STEP 1

Make a loose slip knot and slide it on to the left prong of the loom. From here onwards, whichever prong is on the left side is the working prong, because the loop on this side is the one you will be working into. Loosen the slip knot so that it sits halfway between the prongs. Pass the yarn around the front of the right prong and hold it at the back to tension your work.

CLINIC : HOW CAN I STOP THE LOOPS
✚   : FROM CURLING AND TANGLING
         : WHEN I REMOVE THEM FROM
         : THE LOOM?

Unfortunately, the nature of the hairpin strips means that they are likely to curl. To control this, you can insert a guideline. Thread a contrasting colour yarn through the loops next to the right-hand prong, then take it over the top and down the opposite side. Tie off the yarn loosely at the bottom to secure.

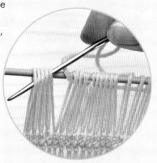

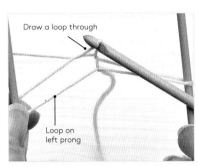

Draw a loop through

Loop on
left prong

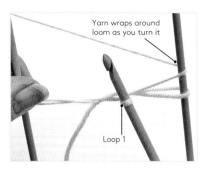

Yarn wraps around
loom as you turn it

Loop 1

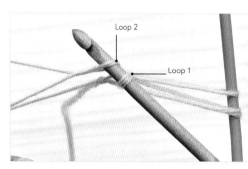

Loop 2

Loop 1

STEP 2
Insert the crochet hook into the loop on the working prong and draw a loop of yarn through. Make one chain to complete the first stitch.

STEP 3
Now the loom must be turned. Keeping the loop on the hook, pass the hook through the middle of the two prongs to the back and turn the loom so that the right prong comes towards you (clockwise). Allow the yarn to wrap around the loom as you turn.

STEP 4
With the hook at the front and tensioning the yarn at the back of the work, insert the hook into the loop on the left-hand prong, wrap the yarn over and draw it through. There are now two loops on the hook.

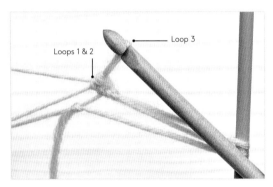

Loop 3

Loops 1 & 2

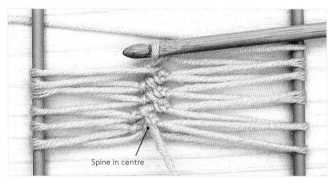

Spine in centre

STEP 5
Wrap the yarn over the hook and draw it through both loops (just like making a standard double crochet).

STEP 6
Repeat from step 3, always turning the loom in the same direction. Try to keep the spine in the centre.

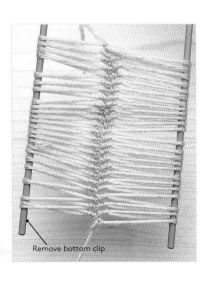

Remove bottom clip

STEP 7
Once the loom is full, cut the yarn and draw the end through the loop on the hook. Remove the bottom clip and slide the strip off the pins.

STEP 8
To work an edging, make a slip knot on the hook, join the yarn to the first hairpin loop on one edge and make a double crochet into the same loop. Make one double crochet in each loop along the edge. Fasten off the yarn and repeat along the opposite edge.

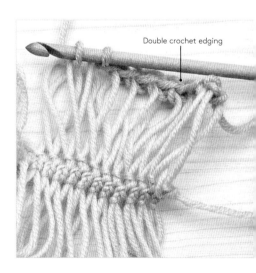

Double crochet edging

Broomstick crochet

This technique creates a light and airy fabric. It was traditionally worked around a broomstick (hence the name), but today a large diameter knitting needle is used instead. The origins of broomstick crochet or lace are uncertain; sometimes called jiffy lace, the technique was popular in postwar America. It has also been known as peacock lace, because the swirly stitches are similar to the eyes on peacock feathers.

UNDERSTANDING THE BASICS

There are a few tools and terms not used in traditional crochet; here they are explained to help you get started.

BROOMSTICK PINS

You will need a large diameter broomstick pin, knitting needle or other round stick. The example shown here was made using a 20mm broomstick pin. The larger the needle size, the bigger the loops will be. The size of the finished piece is determined by the length of the broomstick pin. Wider pieces can be made by sewing strips together.

HOW IT WORKS

Each row is made up of two passes. For the loop pass, a standard crochet hook is used to pull up loops from a base of regular crochet stitches and place them on to the pin. For the return pass, multiple loops are taken off at a time. For each group of loops, a corresponding number of crochet stitches are made so that the stitch count remains the same. The technique is not difficult, but it can be tricky to control the pin and hook at the same time. While it is possible to start by working into the foundation chain, as a beginner it is easier to work one or two rows of standard crochet first. This will give your work a little more stability and make the first loop pass easier to negotiate. Broomstick crochet benefits from blocking to open out the groups of stitches after completion.

BASIC BROOMSTICK CROCHET

This is one of the most basic broomstick stitches, with the pin held in the left hand, but note that some patterns may instruct you to hold the pin in your right hand and some techniques require no pin at all.

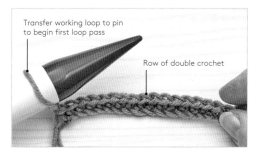

Transfer working loop to pin to begin first loop pass

Row of double crochet

STEP 1

Make the required length of foundation chain. In this example, the foundation chain is a multiple of five because each eyelet is composed of a group of five stitches, plus one turning chain for the first row. Starting in the second chain from the hook, work one row in standard double crochet. Begin the first loop pass by holding the broomstick pin securely in your left hand (some crocheters find it helpful to tuck the end of the pin under their arm), extend the working loop on the crochet hook and then slip it on to the pin.

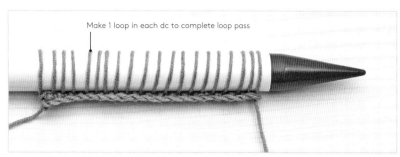

Draw new loop through next dc

Make 1 loop in each dc to complete loop pass

STEP 2
Insert the hook into the next double crochet stitch, wrap the yarn over the hook, draw a loop through, extend the loop and slip it on to the pin.

STEP 3
Continuing along the row from left to right, repeat step 2 until all the stitches have been worked on to the pin. Count the loops to make sure you have a multiple of five.

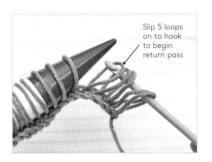

Slip 5 loops on to hook to begin return pass

Draw yarn through 5-loop group, then ch 1

5 dc into 5-loop group

STEP 4
Begin the return pass by slipping the first group of loops off the pin – five loops in this example. Insert the hook through all five loops from right to left.

STEP 5
Wrap the yarn over the hook, draw a loop through the centre of the five-loop group and make one chain to secure.

STEP 6
Make five double crochet into the hole at the centre of the group. (The number of stitches you work into the hole should equal the number of loops in the group.)

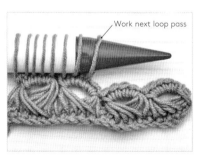

Completed return pass

Work next loop pass

STEP 7
Continue to work along the row, working five loops at a time, to complete the return pass.

STEP 8
To begin the next loop pass, do not turn the work. Extend the working loop on the hook and slide it on to the pin, then repeat from step 2. Continue to work loop and return passes until your work is the required length, finishing with a return pass. Fasten off in the usual way.

SIMPLE IDEAS FOR BROOMSTICK LACE

1 If you prefer, you can vary the pattern by working standard crochet rows in between the broomstick rows.

2 Experiment by working more or fewer loops as you wish, to achieve different effects.

3 As most broomstick crochet begins and ends with a row of standard crochet, it is easy to incorporate it into a project to add visual interest. Try using it as eye-catching end panels on a plain scarf.

Finessing your crochet

As you become more confident and progress from making swatches to small projects, you will come across a range of techniques that can add finesse and polish to your crochet. Some of the simplest ways to improve the finished look of your work are included here.

FOUNDATION ROWS

It is possible to start a piece of crochet without making a foundation chain first. Sometimes called a chainless foundation, this technique produces a flexible, stretchy first row that is neat and visually pleasing. It can be used with any of the basic crochet stitches. At first, you may find it difficult to keep all your stitches the same height because they do not line up next to each other in the same way as a regular first row, and you may find it difficult to see where to work the next stitch. However, with practice you will soon become more proficient.

FOUNDATION DOUBLE CROCHET

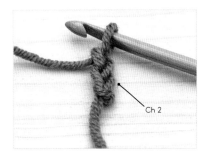

STEP 1
Place a slip knot on the hook and make two chains.

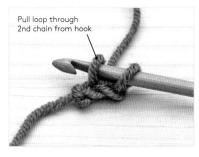

STEP 2
Insert the hook into the second chain from the hook, catch the yarn and draw a loop through.

STEP 3
Make one chain, but make it very loose so that you can work into it easily later. This chain forms the base chain of the foundation stitch.

CLINIC

WHAT CAN I USE THE FOUNDATION ROW TECHNIQUE FOR?

You can replace the standard foundation chain with this technique for any project, except when the first row of crochet includes making extra chains (therefore it is not suitable for mesh, filet or lace projects). The neat and elastic edge it produces makes it an ideal way to begin a garment.

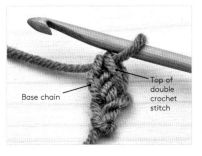

STEP 4
Wrap the yarn over the hook and draw it through both loops on the hook. You now have a double crochet stitch sitting on top of the base chain; it is hard to see this at first because the stitch sits at an angle to the chain (the stitches form on the right, the base chains on the left).

STEP 5
To begin the next foundation stitch, insert the hook as shown under both loops of the base chain of the previous stitch and pull a loop through. Repeat from step 3 to complete the required number of stitches.

FOUNDATION TREBLE CROCHET

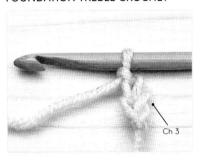

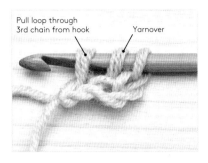

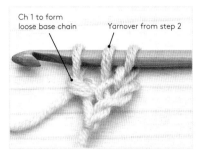

STEP 1
Place a slip knot on the hook and make three chains.

STEP 2
Wrap the yarn over the hook, insert the hook into third chain from the hook and draw a loop through.

STEP 3
Make one chain, making it loose so that you can work into it easily later. This chain forms the base chain of the foundation stitch.

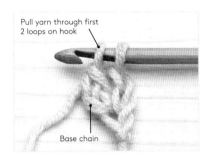

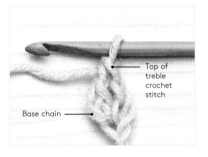

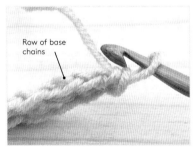

STEP 4
Wrap the yarn over the hook and draw it through the first two loops on the hook.

STEP 5
Wrap the yarn over the hook and draw it through the remaining two loops to complete the first foundation treble crochet stitch. The stitches will form at an angle, with the trebles on the right and the base chains on the left.

STEP 6
To begin the next foundation stitch, wrap the yarn over the hook, insert the hook under both loops of the base chain of the previous stitch and pull a loop through. Repeat from step 3 to complete the required number of stitches. If you turn the work, you will clearly see the loops of the base chains on one side (as shown) and the top loops of the trebles on the other side.

FOUNDATION DOUBLE CROCHET
The base chains under the first row of double crochet stitches form a neat, flexible edge.

FOUNDATION TREBLE CROCHET
This type of foundation produces a very neat edge that many crocheters prefer to a standard foundation chain.

LINKED STITCHES

You may have noticed that the longer turning chains of taller stitches, such as treble crochet, can leave gaps at the side of your work. A simple way to avoid this is to begin each row with a linked stitch. Instead of making the first yarnover, the hook is inserted into one of the turning chains and a loop pulled through the chain. It is also possible to work linked trebles across the row. This can make rows of treble appear less 'gappy', which can be useful when making garments. The resulting fabric has the same drape as treble crochet, but more stability.

LINKED TREBLE IN TURNING CHAIN

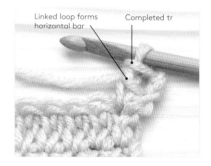

STEP 1
Make the turning chain as usual and insert the hook into the second chain from the hook (you can insert the hook under one or both loops of the chain). Wrap the yarn over the hook and draw a loop through. This forms the link and replaces the first yarnover of the stitch.

STEP 2
Insert the hook into the next stitch of the row in the usual way, yarn over and draw up a loop.

STEP 3
Finish the treble crochet stitch in the usual way by working [yarn over hook, draw through two loops] twice.

LINKED TREBLES ACROSS A ROW

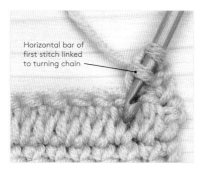

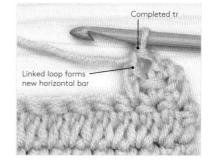

STEP 1
Start with a linked stitch in the turning chain as described above. To make the next stitch, insert the hook into the horizontal bar of the first linked stitch and pull a loop through. This replaces the usual yarnover at the start of a treble and forms the horizontal linking bar.

STEP 2
Insert the hook into the next stitch of the row in the usual way, yarn over and draw a loop through (3 loops on hook). You can now complete the treble in the usual way, working off two loops at a time.

STEP 3
Continue across the row, inserting the hook into the horizontal bar of the previous stitch and pulling a loop through instead of making the usual yarnover to start each treble.

STANDING STITCHES

A standing stitch is a useful way to change colour at the beginning of a row or round, and can be used to replace any of the methods previously taught in this book. The standing stitch replaces the usual turning or starting chain. It is particularly useful when making crochet motifs in the round because there is a crochet stitch rather than a starting chain at the colour change, and many crocheters think that this gives a neater result. This example shows standing treble crochet worked in the round.

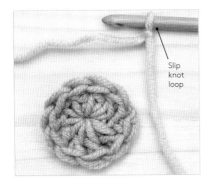

Slip knot loop

STEP 1
Fasten off the old yarn and place a slip knot in the new colour on to the hook. This forms the first working loop of the standing stitch.

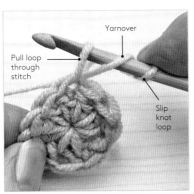

Yarnover

Pull loop through stitch

Slip knot loop

STEP 2
Using a finger to hold the slip knot in place, wrap the yarn over the hook, insert the hook into the stitch where you want to make the join and pull a loop through. Complete the treble crochet in the usual way by working [yarn over, pull through two loops] twice.

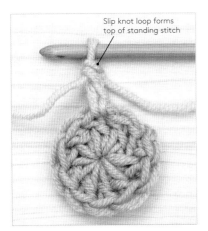

Slip knot loop forms top of standing stitch

STEP 3
The slip knot loop will sit at the top of the completed stitch. The standing stitch starts the round neatly, without a jog between colours, and the yarn tail can be neatly woven in.

8 WAYS TO JOIN A CROCHET COMMUNITY

1 **Visit your local yarn shop.** Yarn shops are not just places to buy yarn. Many of them host social groups and events, or offer clinics where you can ask advice about a project if you run into difficulties.

2 **Search online.** One of the largest online fibre communities is Ravelry (www.ravelry.com). Here you will find crochet enthusiasts sharing patterns, chatting in forums and organising meet-ups and crochet-alongs, where many people work on the same pattern, sharing tips and encouragement. If you are not sure where to start, register on the site and then find one of the designers featured in this book (see page 160), take a look at their work, join their group if they have one and introduce yourself.

3 **Join a knit group.** These have various names, from 'Knit and Natter' to 'Stitch and Bitch', and almost every town has one. Some are run independently, while others are part of the Knitting and Crochet Guild. Despite the name, these groups welcome all kinds of fibre enthusiasts, knitters, crocheters and embroiderers. You may find a listing of local groups in crochet magazines or at your local library or yarn shop.

4 **Attend a fibre event.** Throughout the year you will find fibre-based events all over the world, selling yarns and running classes. These are listed in most crochet magazines, and your local knit group will be able to tell you which ones are nearest to you.

5 **Join a class.** There is always something new to learn in crochet. Joining a class can be great fun and will help you to progress beyond the most basic projects. Look out for classes at your local yarn shop, community college or run by yarn companies. There are even teachers who offer private lessons, so if you are too shy to join a group, you can still progress.

6 **Share your skills.** Passing on your own skills to others can be immensely rewarding, and you will be surprised how much you know. Many schools run craft clubs and welcome volunteers.

7 **Read books and magazines.** Most public libraries have an excellent stock of craft titles, and many knit groups organise informal magazine swaps. These are a great way to find patterns and discover new designers without spending a great deal of money. If you borrow a book and find it useful, you may decide to purchase a copy for yourself.

8 **Register with yarn company websites.** Many yarn companies and online retailers offer free patterns, tutorials and advice.

Quick
start
project:

Tunisian sunglasses case

Sunglasses always seem to fall to the bottom of your bag, so this pretty pastel case will make them easier to spot. The padded nature of Tunisian knit stitch offers protection from scuffs and scratches.

FINISHED SIZE
10 x 20cm (4 x 8in)

TENSION
20 sts and 26 rows = 10cm (4in) square over Tunisian knit stitch

YOU WILL NEED
• 1 x 50g ball of DK-weight wool yarn in each of pink (A), yellow (B) and mauve (C); Tracey used DMC Woolly, 100% merino wool with approx. 125m (136yd) per ball, in 041 (A), 092 (B) and 061 (C), but any DK yarn can be substituted
• 4mm Tunisian crochet hook
• Yarn needle

ABBREVIATIONS AND TECHNIQUES
ch = chain (page 18)
dc = double crochet (page 23)
RS = right side
st(s) = stitch(es)
tr = treble crochet (page 25)
yo = yarn over
Tunisian knit stitch (page 143)
Joining yarn (page 32)
Backstitch (page 43)
Increasing (page 37)
Single slip stitch cord (page 120)

PATTERN NOTES
• Each row consists of a Tunisian forward pass and return pass. Work a standard forward pass for the foundation row as instructed in the pattern; work a Tunisian knit stitch forward pass for all subsequent rows. Work the return pass throughout as follows: [ch 1, yo, pull through 2 loops] to end. The first loop on the hook counts as a stitch.
• Work the colour changes on the last yarnover of a return pass as follows: work to last 2 loops, wrap new yarn colour over hook, pull through both loops. The next forward pass begins with the new colour. Unless specified otherwise, carry unused yarn up the side of the work between stripes.

SUNGLASSES CASE
Foundation chain: Using A, ch 40.
Foundation row: Starting in second ch from hook, [insert hook through ch, yo, draw loop through] to end, do not turn. Make a standard return pass to complete row. (40 sts)
Continue by working Tunisian knit stitch for 40 rows using colours indicated.
Rows 1–14: Yarn A.
Cut yarn A.
Rows 15–16: Yarn B.
Rows 17–18: Yarn C.
Rows 19–30: Repeat rows 15–18 three times more.
Rows 31–32: Yarn B.
Cut yarns B and C.
Rows 33–40: Yarn A.
Row 41: 1 dc in each st to end, turn. (40 sts)
Row 42 (eyelet row): Ch 3 (counts as 1 tr), skip first dc, 1 tr in each st to end.
Fasten off.
With RS together and using backstitch, fold in half lengthways and sew long sides together, then refold with seam down centre back and sew bottom seam. Turn RS out.

FRILLED EDGE
Round 1: Rejoin A to any st, ch 1 (does not count as a stitch), 1 dc in space between each st to end of round. Do not join and do not turn. (40 sts)
Round 2: 2 dc in each st around. (80 sts)
Fasten off and weave in ends.

SLIP STITCH CORD
Foundation chain: Using B, ch 100.
Row 1: Sl st in second ch from hook and in each ch to end.
Fasten off.
Thread cord through eyelets and tie in a bow. Tie a knot in each end of cord and trim.

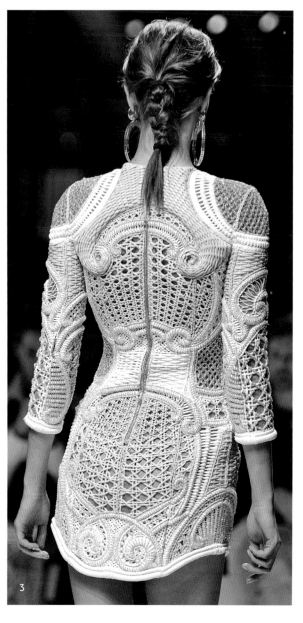

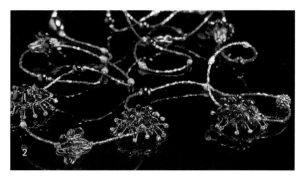

Be inspired

1. BROOMSTICK HAT, MARGARET HUBERT

Today's designers are finding innovative ways to update traditional crochet techniques. A broomstick crochet strip has been transformed into a pretty beanie hat. The picot edging adds stability and a stylish finish.

2. HAIRPIN BEAD NECKLACE, JENNIFER HANSEN

This necklace features two designs of beads made using wire and hairpin crochet. For the bicone beads, garnets are worked into the central stitches of the hairpin strip, then the loops are gathered together at each end. The flower beads have garnets at the centre and seed beads on the loops at one side. These form the petal tips when the opposite loops are gathered together.

3. CROCHET DRESS, BALMAIN AT PARIS FASHION WEEK

Crochet-inspired pieces on the fashion catwalk demonstrate how crochet still captures the imagination of couture designers. This remarkable piece is constructed in a fabric that echoes the openwork of mesh and filet crochet, and shows just how far crochet can be taken in the hands of skilled artisans.

5

6

4. CROCHET DRESS, BALMAIN AT PARIS FASHION WEEK
Highly textured pieces have been joined together to give a crochet doily-inspired effect to this dress. Inspired by the ability to join any crochet shapes together, the structured garment shows how versatile crochet techniques can be.

5. CROCHET BRAID NECKLACE, ELISA ETEMAD FOR ROWAN
Fashion students continue to find innovative ways to explore crochet. The ability to form three-dimensional pieces is shown to great effect in this necklace, which combines wire and yarn to create a unique piece of jewellery.

6. HAIRPIN WIRE BANGLE, JENNIFER HANSEN
This striking bangle combines copper wire with dichroic glass and opalescent seed beads in harmonious colours. The bangle is made from two hairpin strips, with the beads added to the central stitches of each strip. The strips are then joined together along one edge and at the ends to form a circle.

Abbreviations and symbols

Below is a list of the crochet abbreviations and symbols used in this book. Please note that abbreviations and symbols may vary from one pattern publisher to another, so always read the list provided with the pattern you are using before starting a project.

ABBREVIATIONS

Bdc	beaded double crochet
beg	beginning
BO	bobble
BP	back post
ch	chain
CL	cluster
dc	double crochet
dtr	double treble crochet
Exdc	extended double crochet
FP	front post
htr	half treble crochet
PC	popcorn
PS	puff stitch
rep	repeat
RS	right side
sl st	slip stitch
sp	space
SPdc	spike double crochet
st(s)	stitch(es)
tbl	through back loop
tfl	through front loop
tog	together
tr	treble crochet
trtr	triple treble crochet
WS	wrong side
yo	yarn over

GENERAL INSTRUCTIONS

*	Start of repeat
**	End of last repeat
[ ]	Repeat instructions within brackets the stated number of times
( )	Can either be explanatory (counts as 1 tr) or can be read as a group of stitches worked into the same stitch or space (1 tr, ch 2, 1 tr)

CHART SYMBOLS

℃	magic ring
⊖	chain
•	slip stitch
+	double crochet
⊤	half treble crochet
⧊	treble crochet
⧊	double treble crochet
⧊	triple treble crochet
	cluster (e.g. cluster of 4 tr)
	bobble (e.g. bobble of 5 tr)
	popcorn (e.g. popcorn of 5 tr)
	puff stitch (e.g. puff of 5 htr)
⊼	through back loop (e.g. dc tbl)
⊥	through front loop (e.g. dc tfl)
ꙅ	front post (e.g. FPtr)
ꙅ	back post (e.g. BPtr)
✝	extended double crochet
ꙅ	spike double crochet
◆	beaded double crochet
ᖼ	loop stitch
ꟾ	Tunisian simple stitch
ᰧ	Tunisian knit stitch
↗	direction of work

ARRANGEMENT OF SYMBOLS

JOINED AT TOP
A group of symbols joined at the top indicates that these stitches should be worked together at the top, as in cluster stitches, and for decreasing the number of stitches (e.g. tr3tog or 4-tr cluster).

JOINED AT BASE
Symbols joined at the base should all be worked into the same stitch below (e.g. 2 dc in same place or 5-tr shell).

JOINED AT TOP AND BASE
Sometimes a group of stitches are joined at both top and base, making a bobble, popcorn or puff.

ON AN ANGLE
Symbols may be drawn at an angle, depending on the construction of the stitch pattern.

DISTORTED SYMBOLS
Some symbols may be lengthened, curved or spiked, to indicate where the hook is inserted below (e.g. 1 tr in front loop of stitch indicated below).

Glossary

BLOCK
A square, hexagon or other regular shape, worked either in rows or in the round, designed to be repeated and joined together like fabric patchwork. Also known as a motif or medallion.

BLOCKING
Setting a piece of crochet by pinning it out on a flat surface, either wetting it beforehand or spraying or steaming it afterwards, and then allowing to dry.

BOBBLE
Several incomplete stitches, usually treble crochet, worked in the same place as far as the last yarnover and then joined together at the top.

CHAIN SPACE
The space below chain stitches.

CHEVRON
A zigzag formation created by regular increases and decreases.

CLUSTER
Several incomplete stitches worked together so that they join at the top.

EDGING
A decorative trim applied to the edges of crochet or woven fabric. Edgings can be worked separately and sewn on, or they can be worked directly on to the fabric.

FAN
Like a shell, but worked over several rows or into a chain space so that the stitches fan out more.

FILET CROCHET
A regular mesh grid with certain holes filled by extra stitches to form a pattern.

FOUNDATION CHAIN
A length of chain stitches that forms the base for a piece of crochet.

FOUNDATION ROW
A technique for working the first row of crochet without a foundation chain. Some designers also use the term to refer to the first row worked into the foundation chain when that row will not be repeated as part of the stitch pattern.

INTARSIA
Multicoloured designs created by using a separate ball of yarn for each colour.

JOIN AS YOU GO
A technique for joining motifs together while working the final round.

MESH
An open stitch pattern created from a regular grid of chain spaces and stitches (usually treble crochet).

MOTIF
Another name for a block, but most commonly worked in the round. Motifs can be regular or irregular in shape.

MULTIPLE
The number of chains to make for the foundation chain expressed as a multiple of a specific number; this allows the design to be scaled up or down as required. A specified number of extra chains is often added after the multiple calculation to allow for the turning chain and/or to balance the design.

OPENWORK
Any stitch pattern that forms an open, lacy crochet fabric.

PATTERN REPEAT
The specific number of rows or rounds needed to complete one stitch pattern.

PICOT
A decorative loop of chains often closed into a ring with a slip stitch.

POPCORN
Several stitches worked in the same place and then folded over and joined together at the top with a chain.

PUFF STITCH
Like a bobble, but using half treble crochet stitches.

RAISED STITCHES
Stitches formed by inserting the hook around the post (or stem) of a stitch.

RELIEF STITCHES
Stitches worked over other stitches to create pattern and texture.

SHELL
Several stitches worked into the same place to create a shell or scallop shape.

SPIKE STITCH
A stitch worked by inserting the hook one or more rows below the normal position.

STANDING STITCH
Working the first stitch of a row or round without a turning or starting chain.

STARTING CHAIN
The name for a turning chain when working in the round.

STITCH PATTERN
A sequence or combination of stitches repeated over and over again to create a piece of crochet fabric.

SURFACE CROCHET
Decorative stitches worked on top of a crochet background.

TAPESTRY CROCHET
Multicoloured designs created by carrying yarns along the wrong side of the work when not in use, rather than using separate balls like intarsia. Also known as jacquard crochet.

TENSION
The number of stitches and rows to a given measurement, usually 10cm (4in) square, with a suggested hook size.

TRELLIS
Like mesh, but with longer chains that curve upwards to form arches.

TUBULAR CROCHET
A method of working in the round to make crochet tubes or cylinders.

TURNING CHAIN
A number of chains worked at the beginning of a row to bring the hook up to the correct height for the next stitch that is being worked.

WAVE
Like a chevron, but with softer points.

YARNOVER
Yarn wrapped over the hook.

Index

Credits

Quarto would like to thank and acknowledge the following designers for kindly supplying images of their work for inclusion in this book. Particular thanks to Ali Campbell, Stephanie Lau, Leonie Morgan and Maaike van Koert for contributing the guest designer projects, and to Bláithín for modelling the child's bag on page 109.

AMY ASTLE
www.littledoolally.com
pages 52, 114

BALMAIN
Bukajlo Frederic/Sipa/Rex Shutterstock
pages 154, 155

ALI CAMPBELL
www.gethookedoncrochet.co.uk
pages 50-51 (project)

KATE GREEN
www.flourishandfly.co.uk
pages 81, 136: Used with permission by
www.atergcrochet.etsy.com

RASA GRIGAITE
www.esty.com/shops/FallingDew
pages 53, 80, 114

JENNIFER HANSEN
www.stitchdiva.com
pages 154, 155: Designs first appeared in
Crochet Jewellery, a Quarto publication

SIDSEL J. HØIVIK
pages 81, 136
• Facebook, Instagram and webshop:
  sidselhoivik.no
• Photography by Anne Helene Gjelstad:
  www.annehelenegjelstad.com
• Facebook: Anne Helene Gjelstad
  Photography
• Instagram: annehelenegjelstad
• The photographs first appeared in
  Lekre masker og lekne sting, published
  by Gyldendal Norsk Forlag, 2013
• Sidsel J. Høivik and Anne Helene
  Gjelstad are also the team behind
  Vakker strikk til alle årstider, published
  by Gyldendal Norsk Forlag, 2015

MARGARET HUBERT
page 154: Design first appeared in
The Complete Photo Guide to Crochet,
2nd edition, published by Creative
Publishing International, a division of
Quarto Publishing Group USA, Inc.

STEPHANIE LAU
www.AllAboutAmi.com
pages 52, 53, 76-79 (project), 80

LEONIE MORGAN
www.leoniemorgan.com
pages 53, 133-135 (project), 115

DAVID SOARES OLIVEIRA
www.etsy.com/pt/people/entrelacadas
pages 81

SANDRA PAUL
www.cherryheart.co.uk
pages 80, 81, 137

ROWAN
www.knitrowan.com
pages 114, 115, 137, 155

TRACEY TODHUNTER
www.grannycoolcrochet.com
• page 52: Used with permission by
  Victoria Magnus/Eden Cottage Yarns:
  www.edencottageyarns.co.uk
• page 53: Used with permission by Britt
  Spring/Inside Crochet magazine 2013:
  www.brittspring.com
  www.insidecrochet.co.uk
• page 6: Author photograph by
  Andrea Ellsion: www.andreaellison
  photography.com

MAAIKE VAN KOERT
www.creJJtion.com
pages 110-113 (project), 114, 115, 136, 137

Photographs on the 'Be inspired' pages are used with permission of the above contributors. All other images are the copyright of Quarto Publishing plc. While every effort has been made to credit contributors, Quarto would like to apologise should there have been any omissions or errors – and would be pleased to make the appropriate correction for future editions of the book.

SUPPLIER
Special thanks to DMC for providing yarns for use in this book. For DMC crochet threads (Natura and Woolly), patterns, etc, contact:

DMC Creative World Ltd
Unit 21 Warren Park Way
Warrens Park
Enderby
Leicester LE19 4SA
United Kingdom
0116 275 4000
www.dmccreative.co.uk
www.dmc.com

AUTHOR'S ACKNOWLEDGEMENTS
Creating this book has been a team effort. Special mention must go to Michelle, Jackie, Moira, Phil and the whole team at Quarto for their patience, creativity and good humour. Thank you for making the whole process go so smoothly.

Thank you to all my crochet pupils and the ladies of Frodsham Knit and Natter who have tested patterns, offered suggestions and provided coffee and a listening ear whenever needed. Thank you especially to Ali, Michelle, Debbie, Julia and Helen – your constant cheerleading and coffee breaks are part of the reason this book has made it to publication.

Thank you to my family: Colin, for putting up with a yarn and hook filled house; my amazing daughter Nikki who may one day swap her sewing needle for a crochet hook; and my mother-in-law Betty, whose crochet and knit filled home is a constant source of inspiration.

And finally to Sarah, Emma and all the fellow designers who first encouraged me to submit my designs for publication – thank you!